Across the Curriculum

with Favorite Authors

Roald Dahl

Written by Caroline Nakajima

Illustrated by Mathew Erny

Teacher Created Materials, Inc.
P.O. Box 1040
Huntington Beach, CA 92647
©*1994 Teacher Created Materials, Inc.*
Made in U.S.A.
ISBN-1-55734-453-1

The classroom teacher may reproduce copies of materials in this book for classroom use only. The reproduction of any part for an entire school or school system is strictly prohibited. No part of this publication may be transmitted, stored, or recorded in any form without written permission from the publisher.

Table of Contents

Introduction

Our teaching is enriched daily by the wealth of outstanding authors who give us words and pictures to engage, motivate, and inspire our students. Through these authors, our students become acquainted with worlds and ideas beyond their own and emerge as more aware, active, and enthusiastic readers.

In this author series, one author is spotlighted in each resource book. Teachers and students have the opportunity to participate in an in-depth study of each author's work and style.

In this book you will find:

- Lesson plan overview

- Biographical information for a closer look at the author's life, style, motivations, and place in literary history

- Ways to design a classroom to generate interest in the author

- Cross-curricular lessons according to this format:
  - ✓ *Book summaries*
  - ✓ *Before reading the book ideas*
  - ✓ *During reading the book ideas*
  - ✓ *After reading the book ideas*

- A culminating activity to showcase the students' involvement with the author

- Critical thinking activities

- A bibliography and answer key

We are confident the author's approach to studying literature will be a satisfying experience for you and your students!

Overview for Roald Dahl Unit of Study

Introduction to Roald Dahl

- Have students brainstorm what they think makes a good writer. What are some titles of favorite books? What makes a book enjoyable to read? What must an author do to achieve interest?

- Present the six books to be read in this study unit and explain that all of them were written by Roald Dahl. (Show his picture, page 6.)

- Read together the background information about the author. (page 7)

- Discuss what things in his life may have contributed to his success as a writer of children's stories.

- Have students read the books in the order in which they were written (as they are presented in this book). Reading them in that order is helpful in seeing the changes in Dahl's style of storytelling. In addition, reading *Boy Tales of Childhood* last serves to pull all of his prior works together by discovering relationships between his experiences, attitudes, stories, and characters.

Reading the Books

- Present the "Before the Book," "During the Book," and "After the Book" activities you find most appropriate for your students.

- The chapters have been grouped into blocks that follow the storyline, but shorter reading assignments are fine.

- Use Reading Journals for students to write ideas and responses about the stories. Quotes from each book are given and can be used as topics for journals, essays, or discussions.

- As projects are completed, display them in the "Roald Dahl Corner."

Culminating Activities

- Analyze and evaluate Dahl as a writer of children's books.

- Have a Roald Dahl Festival. Invite students from other classrooms to view the character display, listen to selected Reader's Theater presentations, and watch favorite scenes acted out.

Roald Dahl Corner

Designate a reading corner of the classroom as the Roald Dahl Corner.

- Display as many of Dahl's books as are available to you, including those to be read for this study unit.

- Post a copy of Dahl's enlarged picture on a bulletin board.

- Set aside one spot to highlight the particular book being read at the time.

- Have students print their favorite quotes from their reading onto uniform size cards to post around Dahl's picture, adding quotes as books are read.

- Plan space for displaying students' various projects associated with their reading activities, especially a display of all the characters from his books. Some projects can hang on strings from the ceiling.

Roald Dahl

About the Author

Roald (Roo-aal) Dahl was born September 13, 1916, in Llandaff, South Wales, to Norwegian parents, Harald and Sofie (Hesselberg) Dahl. After graduating from Repton School in 1933, he went to work for Shell Oil Company of East Africa until World War II started in 1939. He then served in the Royal Air Force as a fighter pilot and became a Wing Commander. In 1940 Dahl's plane was hit by machine gun fire, and he was severely injured. He was rescued by a fellow pilot and took six months to recover. Although Dahl rejoined his squadron in Greece in the spring of 1941, the pain from his head and back injuries grew worse so that he had to be sent back to England on the disabled list.

Dahl was then reassigned to Washington, D.C., as an assistant air attaché. It was there that he accidentally began his career as a writer. One day while Dahl was in his office, C.S. Forester came to ask if he could interview him for a piece he was writing for *The Saturday Evening Post* because he had "seen action" in the war. Forester took Dahl to lunch with the intention of taking notes about his most exciting war experience. However, Forester was having difficulty taking notes while eating, so Dahl offered to write down some notes and send them to him. The notes ended up being a story which he called "A Piece of Cake." Forester sent the story to *The Saturday Evening Post* under Dahl's name. The Post liked the story and paid Dahl $1,000 and then signed him to write others. Soon his stories were being published in several other magazines, and his writing career had started.

In 1943 Dahl wrote his first children's book, *The Gremlins*. Eleanor Roosevelt read it to her grandchildren and liked it so much that she invited Dahl to have dinner with her and the President at the White House. They had such a good time that he was invited again, and then the visits extended into weekends at their country house. During those visits, Dahl had the unique opportunity to talk with President Franklin Roosevelt about world events as casually as one might have a conversation with an old friend. It was an exciting experience for him.

In 1945, Dahl returned to England and moved into his mother's cottage in Buckinghamshire. In addition to writing, he spent time on his interests in wines, antiques, paintings, and breeding and racing greyhounds.

Seven years later he met actress Patricia Neal, and they married on July 2, 1953. They moved to New York because Pat was working in a play, but they spent their summers in England. They had five children: Olivia (deceased), Tessa, Theo, Ophelia, and Lucy.

James and the Giant Peach was written in 1961. It was the first children's book he had written since *The Gremlins*. Until that time, Dahl had written only short stories and plays for adults. But when Olivia was born, he began making up stories to tell her each night at bedtime. He said, "Had I not had children of my own, I would have never written books for children, nor would I have been capable of doing so." Dahl had some very definite ideas about what children liked to read which were supported by the success of his books. However, some critics considered his work too violent for use in libraries and schools.

Dahl's life was not always an easy one. He had to deal with much serious and tragic illness in his family. Theo had hydrocephalus as a young boy due to multiple head injuries he suffered in an accident as an infant. Olivia died at age 7 from measles encephalitis. His wife suffered three cerebral hemorrhages. Then he had to undergo two spinal operations for crippling back pains. In fact, throughout his life, Dahl had eight major operations and countless smaller ones. Through it all, he always kept a wonderful perspective on life which shines through in his writing.

On November 23, 1990, Roald Dahl died of an infection in Oxford, England. He was an author and screenwriter whose awards include: Edgar Allan Poe Award from the Mystery Writers of America in 1954, 1959, and 1980 for being a "master of the macabre and the surprise denouement"; Federation of Children's Book Groups Award, 1983; Whitbread Award, 1983; and World Fantasy Convention Award, 1983. He had quite a distinguished career for a person who started out having no thoughts of being a writer.

James and the Giant Peach

by Roald Dahl

James Henry Trotter was a happy little boy until he was four years old. Then one day both his parents were eaten up by a rhinoceros that escaped from the London Zoo, and his life completely changed. James was sent to live with his Aunts Sponge and Spiker who were lazy and cruel. He suffered with them for three miserable years, and just when he thought he could not bear it any longer, something magical happened. A strange little man appeared and gave James some green crystals, saying that wonderful things would come from them.

Indeed, the magic crystals created a giant peach that had inside it a group of giants: a grasshopper, centipede, ladybug, spider, silkworm, earthworm, and glowworm! James joined them, and off they went on an adventure across the ocean. They encountered sharks that threatened to end their voyage but were able to escape with the help of some quick thinking by James and hundreds of seagulls. Next, their trip was interrupted by Cloud-Men who used all their weather weapons on them. Nevertheless, they finally reached land and discovered that they had landed in New York City. Although they were at first mistaken for visitors from outer space, they were given a great welcome, and eventually, all of the travelers found success and happiness.

James and the Giant Peach

Before the Book

If peaches are in season, bring some in so that students have a chance to examine them thoroughly. Discuss how they look, feel, smell, and taste. Draw attention to a peach's parts: the stem, the skin, the flesh, and the stone. Record students' reactions on chart paper and save them for the Peach Shape Poem activity after Chapter 7. Show pictures of a peach tree, its leaves, the blossoms, and how the peach grows.

Give a little background about the peach. Peaches are native to China where they grow wild and where farmers have grown them for more than 4,000 years. Chinese legends about the peach tell of its life preserving powers. Anyone who ate a peach was not supposed to die, or at least it would prevent the body from decaying. One legend tells of a peach tree in the garden of a fairy queen which bore fruit only once in 3,000 years. Anyone who picked one of those fruits would live forever.

Traders took peach stones from China to other parts of the world, first to northern India, southeastern Russia, and Persia (now Iran). Next, the peach was taken to other parts of Europe and finally reached England in the 1500's. By that time, Spain had already brought peaches to Mexico and Central America, and North American Indians began to cultivate and spread them throughout the continent.

During the Book

Chapters 1-8

- Chapter 1: Discuss the way Aunt Sponge and Aunt Spiker treated James. How did he feel? Write a letter to James to try to help him cope with his situation. (page 12)

- Chapter 2: Change the aunts' poem to reflect your view of them. (page 13)

- Chapter 3: Draw a picture of what you think the little old man looks like. (page 14)

- Chapter 4: What do you think would have happened if James had followed the old man's instructions instead of dropping the bag on the ground?

James and the Giant Peach

During the Book *(cont.)*

- Chapter 5: "Good heavens," thought James. "What is going to happen in that case if they do meet an earthworm? Or a centipede? Or a spider? And what if they do go into the roots of the peach tree?" Discuss students' predictions about what will happen.

- Chapter 7: Use the words and phrases from the pre-reading activity about peaches and write a Peach Shape Poem. (page 15)

Chapters 9-16

- Chapters 9-10: Ask students what they think James will find inside the peach.

- Chapters 11-13: Learn about invertebrates and discuss whether or not all of these animals in the story are insects. Compare what students learn from their research to the information Dahl gives in the story. Have students identify and label each animal. (page 16)

- Chapter 14: Use the Centipede's Poem for a Reader's Theater activity.

- Chapter 15: Discuss the students' reactions to what happened to the aunts.

- Chapter 16: Ask students to watch for a special reference.

Chapters 17-25

- Chapter 18: Use the Centipede's Song as another Reader's Theater opportunity.

- Chapter 19: Learn about sharks. Could they have behaved as Dahl depicted them?

- Chapter 20: Discuss the plausibility of James's plan.

- Chapter 23: The captain of the ship used many different words to describe the big creatures. Have students practice using synonyms. (page 18)

- Chapter 24: If it is available, bring a violin in to show the class how it makes music. Possibly someone in the class plays the instrument. Then compare how the violin works to the way the grasshopper makes sound. (page 19)

Chapters 26-32

- Chapter 27: Learn about weather. What really causes clouds, snow, and hail?

- Chapter 28: Learn about color and rainbows. Use the worksheet on page 20 to make your own rainbow.

- Chapter 29: Brainstorm together to come up with a solution to Centipede's problem.

10   © *1994 Teacher Created Materials, Inc.*

James and the Giant Peach

During the Book *(cont.)*

Chapters 33-39

- Chapters 33-36: Point of view. Discuss how the events of the Giant Peach landing in New York made the peach group very happy, but it made the New York people afraid. Have students give examples of other events that might have opposing reactions.

After the Book

- Have students work in small groups and choose a "newsworthy" event from the story to report on the TV news. They might want to make it a "late-breaking bulletin" that interrupts the regular programming, or a feature story, or a human interest item. Remind them to cover all the "W" questions: who, what, when, where, and why.

- Discuss with students how a story is made up of a series of events and how one event leads to another. As in real life, one event occurring differently could change one's entire life.

- Diagram the story of *James and the Giant Peach.* (page 21)

- Have students consider how James's life might have been different if a certain event had changed. (page 22)

- Have students create a scrapbook for James. They can draw pictures, paste in items that might be mementos, and write in explanations that he could keep as a remembrance of his great adventure.

- If *National Geographic* had contacted James before he left on his journey, they would have wanted some close-up photographs of the natural wonders he encountered. Have students choose one subject from the story that *National Geographic* would want to feature in its magazine. Using charcoal for black and white photographs or pastels for color, have students draw a series of pictures of one subject James might have photographed if he had taken a camera.

- Complete the Character Descriptions. (pages 23 and 24)

- Comment on the quotes taken from the book. (page 25)

- Make a class Peach Recipes Book. Peaches are used in all kinds of recipes: jams, salads, sauces, desserts. Include a peach recipe from each student and have each student make an illustration to go with the recipe. (page 26)

Support

Poor James was treated so cruelly by his aunts. He was extremely sad and lonely. Be his friend and write him a letter to help him cope with his situation.

Dear James,

_____

_____

_____

_____

_____

_____

_____

_____

_____

_____

_____

_____

_____

_____

_____

_____

_____

_____

_____

Different Perspectives

Aunt Sponge and Aunt Spiker have a view of themselves quite different from how we see them. Using the aunts' poem, change the words to reflect the truth.

"I look and smell," Aunt Sponge declared, "as_____

as a _____ !

Just feast your eyes upon my face, observe my _____

_____ !

Behold my _____ _____

_____ !

And if I take off both my socks

You'll see my _____ _____."

"But don't forget," Aunt Spiker cried, "how much your tummy shows!"

Aunt Sponge went red. Aunt Spiker said, "My sweet, you cannot win,

Behold MY _____ _____

_____ , my _____ ,

my_____ _____!

Oh, _____ me! How I _____

My _____ looks! And please ignore

The pimple on my chin."

"My dear old trout!" Aunt Sponge cried out, "You're only bones and skin!"

"Such _____ as I possess can only truly shine

In _____!" Aunt Sponge declared. "Oh, wouldn't that

be _____ !

I'd _____ all the nation's _____ !

They'd give me all the _____ _____ .

The _____ would all _____ !"

"I think you'd make," Aunt Spiker said, "a _____

_____ !"

Imaginative Characters

Read again the description of the little old man. What are some words and phrases used to describe him?

_____   _____   _____

_____   _____   _____

Use your imagination and draw a picture of what he must have looked like.

Shape Poem

A shape poem is one where words and phrases that describe an object are written in the shape of that object. For example:

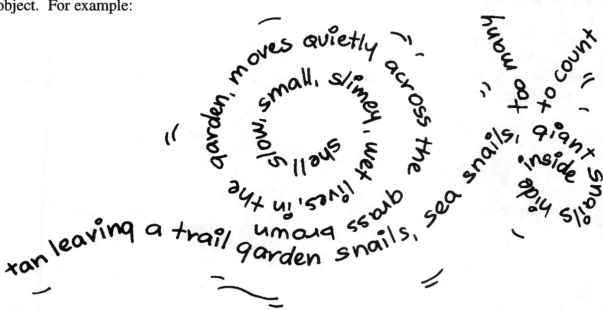

Go back to the chart on which you wrote your reactions to the peach before starting the book. Use them along with other words and phrases that describe a peach to write a Peach Shape Poem.

Peach Creatures

Research the creatures that are in the peach. Insects have three body parts and six legs. Are these all insects? Which ones are?

_____

Identify, label, and color these diagrams of the glowworm, centipede, earthworm, ladybug, grasshopper, spider, and silkworm.

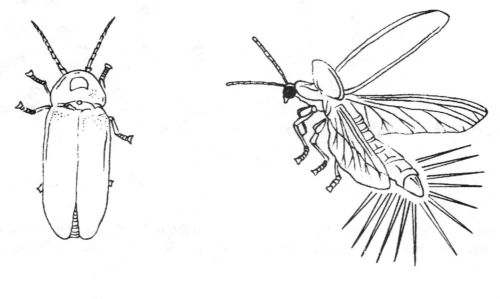

_____

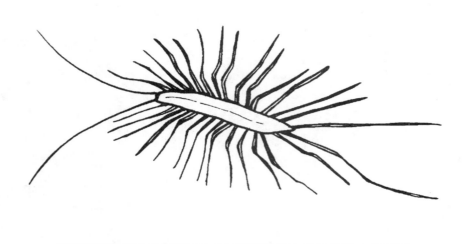

_____

Peach Creatures (cont.)

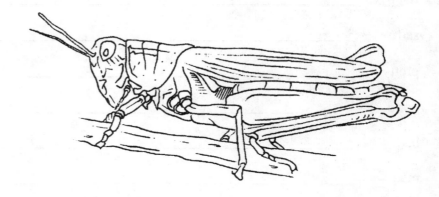

_____

_____   _____

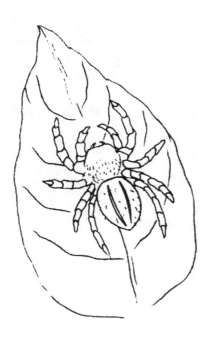

_____   _____

Synonyms

The captain used many different words for big: giant, colossal, mammoth, enormous. These are synonyms. You can make your own writing more interesting by using synonyms for common or overused words. Next to each word below, write three synonyms.

small   _____   _____   _____

nice   _____   _____   _____

funny   _____   _____   _____

happy   _____   _____   _____

sad   _____   _____   _____

pretty   _____   _____   _____

good   _____   _____   _____

bad   _____   _____   _____

mad   _____   _____   _____

Add two words in front of each of the following items to create a better mental image, to change them from the ordinary into the extraordinary.

_____   _____   car

_____   _____   tree

_____   _____   ice cream cone

_____   _____   girl

_____   _____   apple

_____   _____   book

Violin vs. Grasshopper

"And what a wonderful instrument the Old-Green Grasshopper was playing upon. It was like a violin!"

Directions: Compare the violin and the grasshopper after filling in their parts.

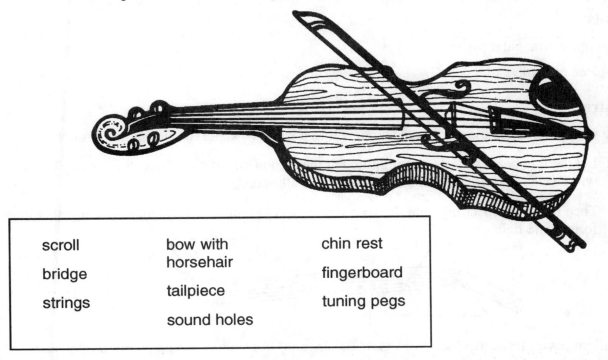

scroll	bow with horsehair	chin rest
bridge	tailpiece	fingerboard
strings	sound holes	tuning pegs

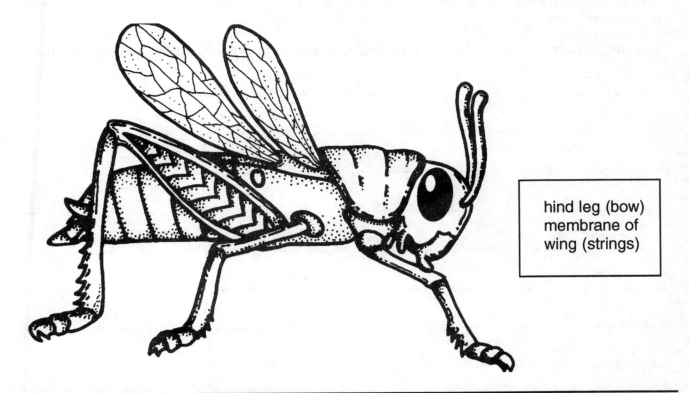

hind leg (bow)
membrane of
wing (strings)

Rainbows

White light is actually a mixture of many colors. If the white light passes through a prism, the light spreads out, and you are able to see the spectrum of colors that make up the light.

Materials:

- two glass triangular prisms
- a piece of cardboard

Procedure:

1. Cut a thin slit in the cardboard and tape it to a window where the sun shines through.

2. Let the thin beam of light coming through the cardboard slit pass through a prism. The light will change into a spectrum of colors on the wall or ceiling.

3. Then focus the spectrum onto the second prism. The colors should come back together to form white light.

When sunlight passes through water droplets in the air (rain), it becomes a rainbow in the sky because the water droplets act like a prism. You may have noticed the same effect with a water hose. Using a nozzle, make a fine spray of water and stand with the sun to your back. You will see that you made your own rainbow.

Do some research and find out why we see colors all around us and what makes things appear black.

_____

_____

_____

_____

_____

_____

_____

_____

Story Diagram

Choose the most significant events from the story and draw pictures of them. Then write one sentence to explain each one.

1	2	3	4

5	6	7	8

What would have happened if...

James's life could have been very different if certain events had taken another path. Use your imagination and consider the following possibilities:

* James's parents had not been killed?

* Aunt Sponge and Aunt Spiker had been kind and gentle people?

* James had actually followed the old man's instructions and swallowed the little green crystals?

* the peach had been a potato or some other food?

* the peach had sunk in the ocean?

* the Cloud-Men had captured James and his friends?

* the people of New York had attacked the Giant Peach?

* James had been alone in the peach?

Choose one of the above and write your new version of James's adventure.

Character Descriptions

Find words and phrases Dahl used to create a mental image of each of his characters. Note the page(s) on which you found the words. Then rate each character on a scale 1 to 5 on how much you like the character as a person.

James   _____

_____

Dislike   1   2   3   4   5   Like

Aunt Sponge   _____

_____

Dislike   1   2   3   4   5   Like

Aunt Spiker   _____

_____

Dislike   1   2   3   4   5   Like

Centipede   _____

_____

Dislike   1   2   3   4   5   Like

Spider   _____

_____

Dislike   1   2   3   4   5   Like

Character Descriptions *(cont.)*

Grasshopper   _____

_____

Dislike   1   2   3   4   5   Like

Earthworm   _____

_____

Dislike   1   2   3   4   5   Like

Ladybug   _____

_____

Dislike   1   2   3   4   5   Like

Glowworm   _____

_____

Dislike   1   2   3   4   5   Like

Silkworm   _____

_____

Dislike   1   2   3   4   5   Like

What Do You Think?

Comment on the following quotes from the book:

Now this, as you can well imagine, was a rather nasty experience for two such gentle parents. But in the long run it was far nastier for James than it was for them. Their troubles were all over in a jiffy. They are dead and gone in 35 seconds flat. Poor James, on the other hand, was still very much alive, and all at once he found himself alone and frightened in a vast unfriendly world. (page 2)

Great tears began oozing out of James's eyes and rolling down his cheeks. He stopped working and leaned against the chopping-block, overwhelmed by his own unhappiness. (page 9)

And then, my dear, you will feel it churning and boiling in your stomach, and steam will start coming out of your mouth, and immediately after that, marvelous things will start happening to you, fabulous, unbelievable things — and you will never be miserable again in your life. (page 15)

All hope of a happier life had gone completely now. Today and tomorrow and the next day and all the other days as well would be nothing but punishment and pain, unhappiness and despair. (page 18)

Something peculiar is about to happen any moment. He hadn't the faintest idea what it might be, but he could feel it in his bones that something was going to happen soon. (page 20)

Most people — and especially small children — are often quite scared of being out of doors alone in the moonlight. Everything is so deadly quiet, and the shadows are so long and black, and they keep turning into strange shapes that seem to move as you look at them, and the slightest little snap of a twig makes you jump. (page 31)

James stopped and stared at the speakers, his face white with horror. He started to stand up, but his knees were shaking so much he had to sit down again on the floor. He glanced behind him, thinking he could bolt back into the tunnel the way he had come, but the doorway had disappeared. There was now only a solid brown wall behind him. (page 35)

James decided that he rather liked the Centipede. He was obviously a rascal, but what a change it was to hear somebody laughing once in a while. (page 43)

The peach rolled on. And behind it, Aunt Sponge and Aunt Spiker lay ironed out upon the grass as flat and thin and lifeless as a couple of paper dolls cut out of a picture book. (page 54)

This building happened to be a famous factory where they made chocolate, and almost at once a great river of warm melted chocolate came pouring out of the holes in the factory wall. (page 56)

And James Henry Trotter, who once, if you remember, had been the saddest and loneliest little boy that you could find, now had all the friends and playmates in the world. (page 153)

Just Peachy

Name: _____ 's Recipe for _____

Ingredients:

Procedure:

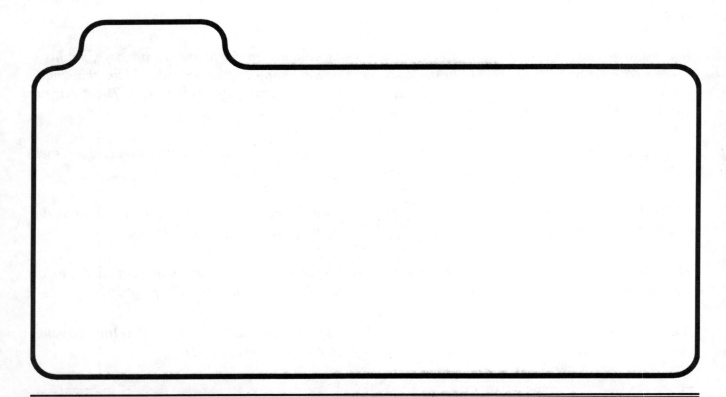

Charlie and the Chocolate Factory

by Roald Dahl

Charlie Bucket lived with his mother, father, and two sets of grandparents. They were very poor and had very little to eat. One day Mr. Willie Wonka announced that he would allow five children to come into his chocolate factory for the first time to learn all his secrets and then provide them with a lifetime supply of chocolates. All they had to do was find a Golden Ticket in a Wonka chocolate bar. Charlie wanted to be one of those children so badly, but having enough money for only one candy a year did not give him much hope.

However, Charlie had the good fortune to find a dollar bill on the street. He decided to spend a small part of it on some Wonka chocolate bars and, miraculously, found the fifth Golden Ticket! Charlie joined Augustus Gloop, Veruca Salt, Violet Beauregarde, and Mike Teavee on a wild adventure into the world of Willie Wonka.

Inside the factory, Charlie saw many unbelievable things, such as the Oompa-Loompas who were little men who did all the work for Mr. Wonka, a chocolate river in a chocolate valley, everlasting gobstoppers, chewing gum meals, and television chocolate that could come right out of your TV. This tour was truly the opportunity of a lifetime. Unfortunately, those who did not follow directions met with disaster. One by one the children disappeared from the group because of their faults, leaving Charlie all alone. As the remaining child, Charlie won the biggest prize of all. He inherited the entire Wonka factory, and his family never had to suffer again.

Charlie and the Chocolate Factory

Before the Book

- Discuss the one thing in the whole world the students would want to eat if they could choose. Talk about how it tastes and makes them feel. Have the students try to "sell" their choice to the others. Ask students what they think Charlie's favorite food is.

During the Book

Chapters 1-4

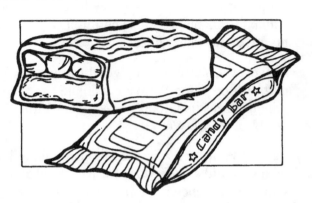

- Chapter 1: Discuss grandparents. What benefits do grandparents add to a young person's life? Brainstorm and list ideas on the board. Interview a grandparent or someone you know who is of that generation. (page 30)

Chapters 5-11

- Chapter 10: Discuss Priorities. What does the word priorities mean? Can priorities change? Is it possible to have everything you want? What if you had only $10 to spend? How would you spend it today? What if you had all the money you wanted? How would you spend it? If you had bought everything you could want or need, then what choices would be left for you to make? (page 31)

- Chapter 11: Question for discussion or journal writing: Do you think Charlie should have sold his ticket for $500 to the woman? His family surely needed the money.

- Learn about Supply and Demand. (page 32)

Chapters 12-20

- Chapter 15: Read *The Kid's Book of Chocolate* by Richard Ammon or other books about chocolate making. Then compare Wonka's candy making process to a real chocolate factory.

- Chapter 18: Read together all the ways that Wonka was called "crazy." Have students brainstorm many words that can describe Willie Wonka, and have them complete the Willie Wonka acrostic. (page 33)

Chapters 21-27

- Have a discussion about TV vs. books. List the pros and cons of each.

- Give students Willie Wonka's TV Message to unscramble. (page 34)

Charlie and the Chocolate Factory

During the Book *(cont.)*

Chapters 28-30

- Ask students to think about where they would like to go if they had access to a Great Glass Elevator like Willie Wonka's. (page 35)

After the Book

- Cause and Effect Discussion: Have students tell what the cause was of the strange events that happened to the children who visited the Wonka Chocolate Factory. Then discuss what lessons for children Mr. Dahl may have had in mind when he created these characters. Do you agree with him? Examine each character and the traits which Mr. Dahl valued or condemned. (page 36)

- Reader's Theater Song: Have groups of students choose an Oompa-Loompa song to read in a Reader's Theater format.

- Art Project: Have students illustrate a room of the candy factory. Let them choose one described in the book or create one of their own. Tell them to include as much detail as possible, name the room, and explain the drawing to the class.

- Essay Assignment: Willie Wonka said: "A grown-up won't listen to me; he won't learn. He will try to do things his own way and not mine." He was explaining why he decided to give his factory to a child. Ask students if they agree with him. Do they find that grown-ups are that way? What experiences have they had that support their view? (page 37)

- Business Plan: Learn about starting a new business. What are the basic steps? Have students write their own business plans. (page 38)

- Story Diagram: Have students diagram *Charlie and the Chocolate Factory*. What are the problems and goals, and how are they resolved? (page 40)

- Character Descriptions: Have students complete the Character Descriptions. (page 41)

- Book Quotes: Comment on the quotes taken from the book. (page 42)

- Chocolate Recipes Book: Chocolate is used in all kinds of recipes: breads/muffins, cookies, cakes, pies, candies, and other treats. Include a recipe from each student that uses chocolate and have students make illustrations to go with their recipes. (page 43)

Senior Citizens

There is much to be learned from talking to grandparents. We can gain a perspective on life different from that which we learn from our parents or friends. Interview a grandparent or someone you know who is of that generation. Use this interview sheet as a guide for asking questions. Then share one or two things you learned from the interview.

Interview Questions

Name of person being interviewed _____

Relation to student _____

When and where were you born? _____

Who was your hero as a child? Why? _____

_____

What do you think has been your most important accomplishment? _____

What do you think is the most interesting change you have seen in your lifetime? _____

_____

_____

Is there anything you miss from the past? _____

What is one bit of advice you have for me? _____

(Add your own questions)

_____

_____

_____

_____

_____

_____

Priorities

What are priorities?_____

Are priorities the same for everyone?_____

How do you decide what your priorities are? _____

For the following questions, first answer for yourself, then write down what you think Charlie might have said.

Think carefully about all the things you would like to have today. If you were given $10 to spend, what would you do with it? (Estimate prices the best you can.)

You:_____

_____

Charlie: _____

_____

Now consider what you would buy if you had all the money you wanted.

You:_____

_____

Charlie: _____

_____

After spending as much money as you wanted, what kinds of choices would be left for you to make?

You:_____

_____

Charlie: _____

_____

Supply and Demand

Supply refers to the amount of a particular item (or goods) available for purchase, and demand refers to how much that item is wanted by the people. To better understand this principle, complete the questions.

What items, or goods, did Willie Wonka supply? _____

_____

What happened to the demand for Wonka's goods when he announced the golden tickets?

_____

Usually, when the demand for something increases, then the supply decreases. Why do you think that would happen?

_____

If the supply becomes scarce, then people are often willing to pay more for it; that is, the price of that item goes up. What happened in the story that is an example of this principle?

_____

After Charlie found the last Golden Ticket, what do you think happened to the demand for Wonka's goods?

_____

When the demand for a product goes down, what do you think will happen to the supply?

_____

If Willie Wonka were left with lots of extra chocolates that were not selling, what do you think he might do to sell them?

_____

_____

Can you think of something in your life where you saw the principle of supply and demand at work?

_____

_____

Willie Wonka

W_____

I_____

L_____

L_____

I_____

E_____

W_____

O_____

N_____

K_____

A_____

Illustrate Willie Wonka.

Wonka's TV Message

Willie Wonka sent a message by TV which was broken up into many pieces but did not get put back together again properly. Unscramble the words and write them as they should be on the TV screen.

TAKING MEET ENJOY NEAR GREAT WONKA PLACES ALONG CHARACTERS. BOOKS CHOCOLATE LIKE WAY READING TO KINDS GLASS BAR RIDE ALONG ELEVATOR WHERE OF OR YOU'LL ALL DISTANT BE TO THE SURE A TAKE TO A IS.

The Great Glass Elevator

If you could take a ride in the Great Glass Elevator, where would you go? What things would you like to see, and whom would you take with you?

Cause and Effect

While on the tour of the Chocolate Factory, many unusual things happened to the children. Below is a list of "effects," that is, things that happened because of something else. Tell what you think was the cause for each of those events.

Cause	**Effect**
_____	Augustus is sucked up a pipe.
_____	Violet turns into a blueberry.
_____	Veruca is thrown into the garbage chute.
_____	Mike shrinks.
_____	Charlie inherits the factory.

What lessons do you think Mr. Dahl was trying to teach with each of these characters?

Augustus Gloop _____

Violet Beauregarde _____

Veruca Salt _____

Mike Teavee _____

Charlie Bucket _____

Do you agree with Mr. Dahl? Why (not)?_____

_____

_____

Grown-ups vs. Children

Willie Wonka said: "A grown-up won't listen to me; he won't learn. He will try to do things his own way and not mine." He was explaining why he decided to give his factory to a child. Do you agree with him? Do you find grown-ups are that way? What experiences have you had that support your view?

Business Plan

Charlie is going to be the owner of a fabulous business. He will learn all about running the business from Mr. Wonka, but what if he had to actually start up the business from the beginning? What might he have to consider?

I. Type of Business and Objectives

What will be sold? _____

Is that a product or a service? _____

What will be the name of the business? _____

What do I (Charlie) hope to accomplish with the business? _____

_____

II. Market Analysis

Who will buy it? _____

Why? _____

III. Production

Where will the business be located? _____

What equipment is needed? _____

What materials and supplies are needed? _____

What kind of labor help do I need? _____

IV. Marketing

How will the product/service be sold? _____

How will it be advertised? _____

What are my plans for development and growth? _____

V. Organization and People

Who will help me run the business? _____

What will be their jobs? _____

VI. Funding

How much is needed for equipment? _____

How much for materials and supplies? _____

What salaries will I have to pay? _____

Where will the money to get started come from? _____

How will I decide how much to charge for my product/service? _____

_____

Business Plan *(cont.)*

Now think of a business for yourself. It can be as simple or complex as you like. For example, you might want to have your own lawn mowing service, or make cookies to sell. You may want to do this by yourself, with a partner, or a small group. Then fill in the same business plan for your business as you did for Charlie.

I. Type of Business and Objectives

What will be sold? _____

Is that a product or a service? _____

What will be the name of the business? _____

What do I hope to accomplish with the business?_____

_____

II. Market Analysis

Who will buy it? _____

Why? _____

III. Production

Where will the business be located? _____

What equipment is needed? _____

What materials and supplies are needed? _____

What kind of labor help do I need? _____

IV. Marketing

How will the product/service be sold? _____

How will it be advertised? _____

What are my plans for development and growth? _____

V. Organization and People

Who will help me run the business? _____

What will be their jobs? _____

VI. Funding

How much is needed for equipment? _____

How much for materials and supplies? _____

What salaries will I have to pay? _____

Where will the money to get started come from? _____

How will I decide how much to charge for my product/service? _____

_____

Story Diagram

| Problem(s) | _____ |

| Goal(s) | _____ |

Event 1 _____

Event 2 _____

Event 3 _____

Event 4 _____

| Resolution | _____ |

Character Descriptions

Find words and phrases Dahl used to create a mental image of each of his characters. Note the page(s) on which you found the words. Then rate each character on a scale of 1 to 5 on how much you like the character as a person.

Charlie _____

_____

Dislike   1   2   3   4   5   Like

Grandpa Joe _____

_____

Dislike   1   2   3   4   5   Like

Augustus Gloop _____

_____

Dislike   1   2   3   4   5   Like

Veruca Salt _____

_____

Dislike   1   2   3   4   5   Like

Violet Beauregard _____

_____

Dislike   1   2   3   4   5   Like

Mike Teavee _____

_____

Dislike   1   2   3   4   5   Like

What Do You Think?

Comment on the following quotes from the book:

Walking to school in the mornings, Charlie could see great slabs of chocolate piled up high in the shop windows, and he would stop and stare and press his nose against the glass, his mouth watering like mad. Many times a day, he would see other children taking creamy candy bars out of their pockets and munching them greedily, and that, of course, was pure torture. (Chapter 1)

Like all extremely old people, he was delicate and weak, and throughout the day he spoke very little. But in the evenings when Charlie, his beloved grandson, was in the room, he seemed in some marvelous way to grow quite young again. (Chapter 2)

"You never know, darling," said Grandma Georgina. "It's your birthday next week. You have as much chance as anybody else." (Referring to Charlie getting one of the Golden Tickets) (Chapter 5)

"He spoils her," Grandpa Joe said. "And no good can ever come from spoiling a child like that, Charlie, you mark my words." (Chapter 6)

But there was one other thing that the grownups also knew, and it was this: that however small the chance might be of striking lucky, the chance was there. (Chapter 7)

All at once, they both saw the funny side of the whole thing, and they burst into peals of laughter. (Chapter 9)

...and because we are all a great deal luckier than we realize, we usually get what we want — or near enough. (Chapter 10)

There was a peculiar floating sensation coming over him, as though he were floating up in the air like a balloon. His feet didn't seem to be touching the ground at all. He could hear his heart thumping away loudly somewhere in his throat. (Chapter 11)

And his eyes — his eyes were most marvelously bright. They seemed to be sparkling and twinkling at you all the time. The whole face, in fact, was alight with fun and laughter. (Chapter 14)

Mr. Wonka himself had suddenly become even more excited than usual, and anyone could see that this was the room he loved best of all. He was hopping about among the saucepans and the machines like a child among his Christmas presents, not knowing which thing to look at first. (Chapter 19)

"...A grownup won't listen to me; he won't learn. He will try to do things his own way and not mine. So I have to have a child. I want a good sensible loving child, one to whom I can tell all my most precious candy-making secrets — while I am still alive." (Chapter 30)

"You mustn't despair!" cried Wonka. "Nothing is impossible! You watch!" (Chapter 30)

"Please don't be frightened," he said. "It's quite safe. And we're going to the most wonderful place in the world!" (Chapter 30)

Chocolate Choices

Name: _____ 's Recipe for _____

Ingredients:

Procedure:

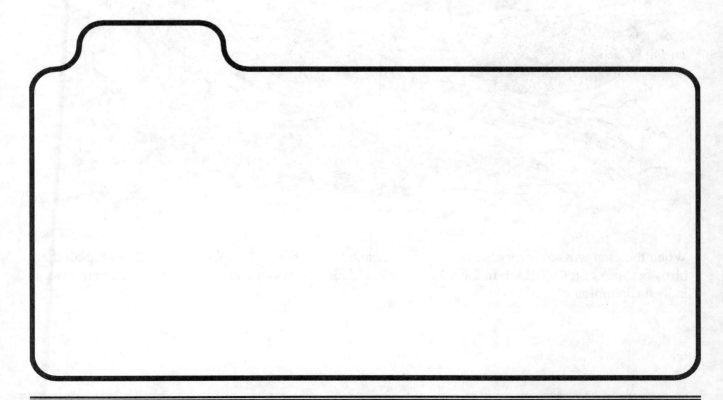

Danny, the Champion of the World

by Roald Dahl

Danny lived with his father in an old gypsy caravan next to the service station his father owned. They had a simple life, and it was an extremely happy one. His father was a good mechanic and taught Danny all about repairing automobiles by the time Danny was seven. He also showed him about building kites, hot air balloons, and all kinds of enjoyable things. In fact, he always seemed to have some kind of surprise up his sleeve.

One day when Danny was nine years old, he learned about his father's "deep, dark secret." His father was a pheasant poacher! Although poaching was not legal, it was an exciting sport, and it seemed almost justified to take a few pheasants from old Mr. Hazell's woods because he was such a selfish and rude person. For that reason, Danny and his dad came up with an outrageous plan to poach Mr. Hazell's 200 pheasants that were being raised for his annual shooting party. Danny thought of a way to catch the 200 pheasants all at once. It was to be the best trick of all.

When the plan worked, everyone in town was ecstatic even though they were not able to keep all the birds because of a tiny glitch in the scheme. Nevertheless, it was a great adventure, and Danny was indeed Champion of the World.

Danny, the Champion of the World

Before the Book

- Have a class discussion and include the following:
  - — Read the title. What do you think made Danny the champion of the world?
  - — Look at the picture on the cover. When do you think this story takes place? What clues are there? Who are the two people?
  - — Of what activity might you consider yourself the champion of the world? Or for what would you like to be a champion?
  - — How do you get to be the best at something?
  - — What is a gypsy caravan?

During the Book

Chapters 1-3

- Chapter 1: Describe Danny's home — all the buildings, land, etc. How does it compare to your home? (page 47)

- Chapter 2: Describe Danny's father. Find words and phrases from the story.
  - — Who is BFG? Tell about one dream you have had. Was it scary? funny? strange? Read Roald Dahl's book *BFG*.

- Chapter 3: Assign demonstration projects. Have students choose a machine, a tool, or a vehicle and demonstrate how it works. They can build a model, make poster diagrams, or bring in the actual object. Explanations should be simple but precise.

  - — Make a kite.
  - — Study hot air balloons. What is their history? How do they work? (page 48)
  - — Discuss being a designing engineer. Working in small groups, design something new or an improved version of an existing object. For example, how can the bicycle, car, or plane be improved, or can you think of an entirely new mode of transportation? How would it work?

Chapters 4-9

- Chapter 4: Topic for discussion or journal writing: Why was Danny scared? Can you relate to the feelings of panic and fear?

- Chapter 5: What were the secret methods?

- Chapter 6: Describe Mr. Victor Hazell.

  - — Use the clues associated with the Austin Seven, or Baby Austin, and figure out what year it is in the story.

- Chapters 7-8: What had happened to Father? Do you think Danny did the right thing?
  - — Do distance-rate-time math problems. (page 49)

Danny, the Champion of the World

During the Book *(cont.)*

- Chapter 9: Describe Doc Spencer. Why did he hate Mr. Hazell? How would you have handled the situation with Mr. Hazell?

Chapters 10-13

- Chapters 10-11: What was Father's great wish? What was Danny's great idea?

- Chapter 12: What bit of educational philosophy does Roald Dahl include here?

    — Each day during the month, have one student prepare an interesting fact to write on the board for students to read that day just like Danny's idea about what his dad might have written for his school. "Did you know?"

- Research something natural found in your area.

- Chapter 13: What kind of person was Danny's mother?

Chapters 14-18

- Chapter 14: Explain all the emotions Danny and his dad felt in these words: fantastic, panic, tense, ecstatic, proud. (page 50)

- Chapter 16: Why was Danny called the Champion of the World?

- Chapters 17-18: What astonishing information did Danny learn about the people of the town? What do you think about that?

    — What did Father decide to buy? Why?

Chapters 19-22

- Chapter 19: Why was the baby crying?

- Discuss the way Dahl is able to make his readers laugh. Have students recall the humorous sight of pheasants flying out from under the baby! Ask students to think of humorous incidents in other books read or movies seen that they can relate to the class. (page 51)

- Chapters 20-22: What do you think about the ending? What was Roald Dahl's message? (page 52)

After the Book

- Explain the Herringbone Story Diagram and have students fill one in for the story of *Danny, the Champion of the World*. (page 53)

- Complete the Character Descriptions. (page 54)

- Comment on the quotes taken from the book. (page 55)

- Danny and his father often enjoyed a late night snack together. It was a relaxing time when they had a chance to talk. Make a class recipe book of Favorite Snacks. (page 56)

Venn Diagram

How does Danny's home (all the buildings land, location, etc.) compare to your own?

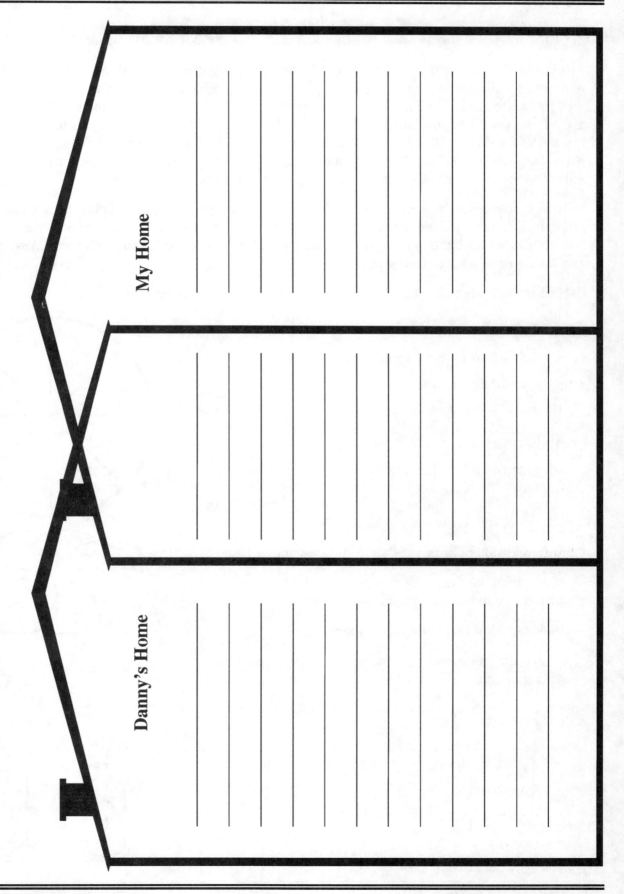

My Home

Danny's Home

Hot Air Balloon

In 1783 in France, the brothers Joseph and Etienne Montgolfier invented the first hot air balloon. They built a fire and inflated a huge linen bag with the hot air which rose from the fire's heat. This linen bag was 100' (30.5 m) in circumference and lined with paper. To demonstrate their balloon to Louis XVI and Marie Antoinette, the Montgolfiers attached a cage with the first passengers inside: a duck, a rooster, and a sheep. This flight lasted eight minutes and went nearly two miles (3.2 km). Soon after, two other men, J.F. Pilatre de Rozier and Marquis D'Arlandes, successfully flew a little more than five miles (8 km) across Paris at a height of about 300' (91.5 m).

However, due to the dangerous nature of the hot air balloon, hydrogen balloons became more prominent in the 19th century. In the 20th century a safer burner fueled by propane was invented which brought the hot air balloon back into popularity. Today hot air ballooning is a sport many people enjoy as a hobby or as a special excursion.

Experiment with hot air. To see that hot air rises, do this simple demonstration:

Materials:

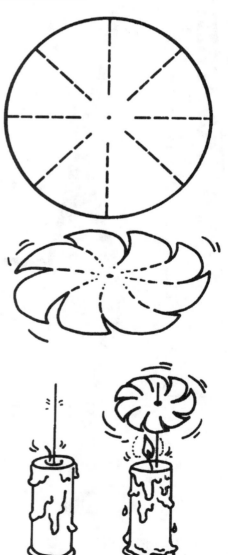

- 2.5" x 2.5" (1 cm x 1 cm) piece of foil
- one candle
- one paper clip

Preparation:

1. Cut the foil into a 2.5" (1 cm) diameter circle, using the pattern. Cut along the dotted lines, leaving the center intact. With a ballpoint pen, make an indentation in the center of the foil without making a hole.

2. Lift one side of each cut flap to form a windmill shape.

3. Straighten out the paper clip into a straight wire and insert it as close to the candlewick as possible.

4. Place the foil gently on top of the paper clip.

5. Light the candle and see the "windmill" spin due to the rising hot air.

Note to the Teacher: Use extreme caution while using a lit candle.

Distance - Rate - Time

The formula for computing distance (d) using rate (r) and time (t) is:

d (miles/km) = r (miles/km per hour) x t (hours).

Using this formula, we can derive formulas for rate and time:

t = d ÷ r and r = d ÷ t.

Use these formulas to answer the following problems.

1. Danny had to go 6.5 miles (10.5 km) to Hazell's Wood. If he is able to walk 3 miles (5 km) per hour, how long will it take him to reach his destination?

2. Using the Baby Austin, how long would the trip take going at an average speed of 25 miles (40 km) per hour? at 40 miles (64.5 km) per hour? Give your answers first in hours and then in minutes.

3. If Danny were driving today, he would be an adult with an up-to-date car. Approximately how fast would he be going if he made the trip in seven minutes? (Be careful not to mix up minutes and hours.)

4. If Danny could take a shortcut walking through the fields, he could cut the distance to Hazell's Woods in half, but he would have to move more slowly at a rate of about 2 miles (3.2 km) per hour. Would it still be better to take the shortcut? What is the time difference?

5. Danny decided to run the first two miles. It took 15 minutes. What was his rate while he was running?

Emotions

Danny and his dad went on a great adventure. Their experience caused them to feel many different emotions during those hours in the woods. The following words and phrases taken from Chapter 14 tell or imply their feelings. Explain each one.

My father was squinting anxiously up at the sun. _____

_____

For although the snakes were still wiggling in my stomach, I wouldn't have swapped places with the King of Arabia at that moment.

_____

That's the fun of the whole thing. _____

I could see my father becoming more and more twitchy. _____

_____

I was very grateful to him for holding my hand. _____

_____

My father was very tense. _____

His face was transfixed in ecstasy. _____

_____

I froze. _____

I could feel a trickle of cold sweat running down one side of my forehead and across my cheek.

_____

This was the moment of danger, the biggest thrill of all. _____

_____

Don't you love this? _____

His face was scarlet and glowing with triumph. _____

I'm proud of you. _____

Humor

Imagine the humorous sight of pheasants flying out from under the baby! Think of a humorous incident from another book or from a movie that you can describe here. Be sure to tell where your incident came from. Then draw your mental image of the incident.

_____

_____

_____

_____

Parenting

Being a parent is hard work. Roald Dahl said that "what a child wants and deserves is a parent who is sparky." What does he mean by that? Do you agree?

_____

_____

Write down some of your own ideas about parenting.

When I become a parent, I will: When I become a parent, I will not:

_____   _____

_____   _____

_____   _____

_____   _____

_____   _____

_____   _____

Herringbone Story Diagram

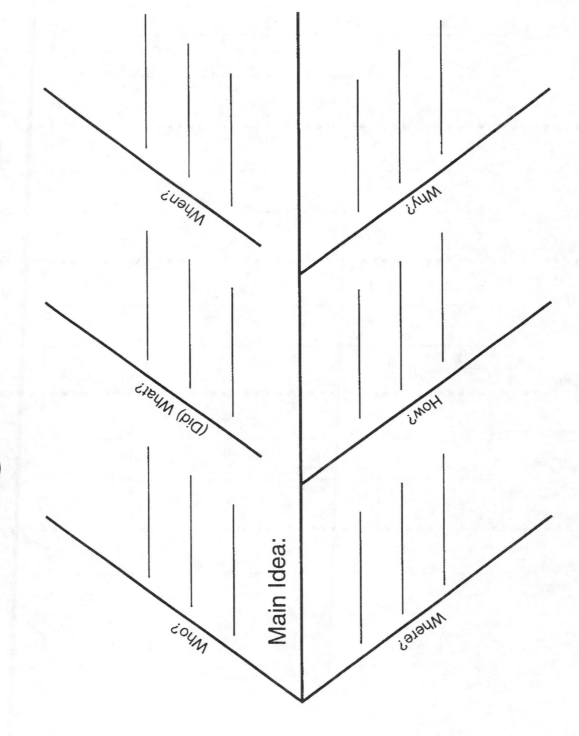

When?

(Did) What?

Who?

Why?

How?

Where?

Main Idea:

Character Descriptions

Find words and phrases Dahl uses to create a mental image of each of his characters. Note the page(s) on which you found the words. Then rate each character on a scale of 1 to 5 on how much you like the character as a person.

Danny
_____

_____

Dislike   1   2   3   4   5   Like

Father
_____

_____

Dislike   1   2   3   4   5   Like

Victor Hazell
_____

_____

Dislike   1   2   3   4   5   Like

Doc Spencer
_____

_____

Dislike   1   2   3   4   5   Like

The Keeper,
Mr. Rabbetts
_____

_____

Dislike   1   2   3   4   5   Like

What Do You Think?

Comment on these quotes:

Most wonderful of all was the feeling that when I went to sleep, my father would still be there, very close to me, sitting in his chair by the fire, or lying in the bunk above my own. (Chapter 1)

It meant he never gave me a fake smile because it is impossible to make your eyes twinkle if you aren't feeling twinkly yourself. A mouth-smile is different. You can fake a mouth-smile anytime you want, simply by moving your lips. I've also learned that a real mouth-smile always has an eye-smile to go with it. So watch out, I say, when someone smiles at you with his mouth but his eyes stay the same. It's sure to be a phony. (Chapter 2)

You will learn as you get older, just as I learned that autumn, that no father is perfect. Grown-ups are complicated creatures, full of quirks and secrets. Some have quirkier quirks and deeper secrets than others, but all of them, including one's own parents, have two or three private habits hidden up their sleeves that would probably make you gasp if you knew about them. (Chapter 4)

...For the first time in my life, I felt a touch of panic...There was a new moon in the sky, and across the road the big meadow lay pale and deserted in the moonlight. The silence was deathly. (Chapter 4)

Most of the really exciting things we do in our lives scare us to death. (Chapter 7)

It's worse than that, William! It's diabolical! Do you know what this means? It means that decent folk like you and me can't even go out and have a little fun at night without risking a broken leg or arm. We might even break our necks! (Chapter 9)

I really loved those morning walks to school with my father. We talked practically the whole time. Mostly it was he who talked and I who listened, and just about everything he said was fascinating. He was a true countryman. (Chapter 12)

...But I'll tell you something very funny about the old bullfrog. He often becomes so pleased with the sound of his own voice that his wife has to nudge him several times before he'll stop his burping and turn around to hug her.
That made me laugh.
Don't laugh too loud, he said, twinkling at me with his eyes. We men are not so very different from the bullfrog. (Chapter 12)

Terrific, I said. And I meant it. For although the snakes were still wiggling in my stomach, I wouldn't have swapped places with the King of Arabia at that moment! (Chapter 14)

Oh, yes you did! And you know what that makes you, my dear boy? It makes you the champion of the world! (Chapter 16)

I was astounded. But I was also rather pleased because now that I knew the great Sergeant Sam was human like the rest of us, perhaps I wouldn't be so scared of him in the future. (Chapter 17)

Those were the greedy ones, the doctor said. It never pays to eat more than your fair share. (Chapter 21)

Favorite Snacks

Name: _____ 's Recipe for _____

Ingredients:

Procedure:

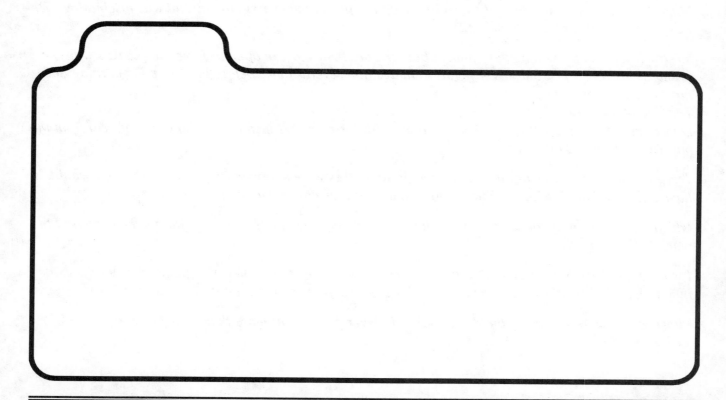

The Witches

by Roald Dahl

A young boy who lives with his Norwegian grandmother learns all about real witches and tells of two encounters he had with a witch. The first time he was lucky and escaped unharmed, but the second encounter changed his life forever.

One day as the boy was working on his treehouse, a strange woman appeared below him. She smiled in an unusual way and offered him a present. Luckily, Grandmother had told him all about witches — how they look and act — so he was alert to her suspicious appearance. He remained in his treehouse for hours until his grandmother finally came looking for him. The woman had disappeared. He never saw her again, but he and his grandmother were extra cautious after that.

The following summer, the boy and his grandmother went on a trip to the south coast of England and stayed at the Hotel Magnificent. He took with him a pair of white mice that his grandmother had given him as a gift, since they were not able to go to Norway as they had originally planned. At the hotel, he wanted to spend time training his pet mice, but the manager would not allow them out of their cage. Not to be stopped, the boy found a large empty ballroom where he thought he could safely work with his mice without being discovered. Unfortunately, the room was reserved for a meeting of a special society of women, and when they began to arrive, the boy hid behind a folding screen in the back of the room.

As he sat and listened, he was horrified to learn that these were not ordinary women. They were witches! He heard their plans for doing away with all the children of England and could hardly believe their plot. The witches discovered him and turned him into a mouse — the same fate that was in store for all the other children. Even though he looked like a mouse, he was still the same person on the inside. He was still able to think and speak as the boy he was before. He escaped from the witches, and with the help of his grandmother, he stopped the witches from carrying out their plans. The only thing he could not change was that he was a mouse for the rest of his life.

The Witches

Before the Book

- Ask students to create a list of how one could recognize a real witch. Then have them share their ideas with the class. You may want to list the most popular ideas on chart paper to compile a class list.

- Take a poll of how many students believe in witches. Ask them to describe a witch—appearance, actions, and where to find them. After reading the book, see if there is a change of opinion. (page 60)

During the Book

Chapters 1-4

- As students read these chapters, have them make notes about any important information regarding witches. (page 61) Then, have students work in small groups to brainstorm ways to find witches. Share the ideas with the whole class and discuss the merits of each plan.

Chapters 5-6

- Discuss the circumstances that led up to the situation in which the boy found himself. Why were they at that particular hotel? Why did he have two pet mice with him? Why was he training them in that ballroom? Why did he faint for a few minutes? What specific clues caused him so much anxiety? Have students make predictions about what will happen next.

Chapters 7-10

- Have students write their reactions to these chapters in their reading journals. What do they think of the Grand High Witch? of her plan? of Bruno's plight?

Chapters 11-12

- Essay or discussion topic: What possible alternatives did the main character have to being caught and turned into a mouse? Were there any? What might you have done?

Chapters 13-16

- Compare and contrast the reactions of Grandmamma and Mr. and Mrs. Jenkins to the discovery of the boys turned to mice. Why do you think they were so different? Which reaction do you think your own parents would have about such news?

Chapters 17-20

- Who came up with the "The Plan"? Why do you think the plan was successful?

Chapters 21-22

- Have students think about their own homes and activities and how they would have to modify things to accommodate them if they were changed into mice.

- Have students research mice. Then give them the Mouse Puzzle to complete. (page 62)

The Witches

After the Book

- Poll the students again about their beliefs in witches to see if there was a change of opinion after reading the story. (page 60)

- Discuss similarities and differences between the witches of Dahl's book and other witches you have read or heard about such as: (page 63)
  — The Witch of the West and Witch of the East in *Wizard of Oz*
  — The witch in *Snow White*
  — The witch in *Hansel and Gretel*
  — The Halloween witch
  — The witch in *Sleeping Beauty*

- Discuss the meaning of "stereotype." What stereotypes do we have of: witches, grandmothers, little boys? In what ways are the witches, grandmamma, and the main character different from the stereotypes? Describe their unique characteristics as well as telling how they are typical. (page 64)

- Act out a scene from the book.

- Essay topic: Did you like the ending? Were you surprised? How would you change it?

- Diagram the story of *The Witches* using the W diagram. (page 65)

- Complete the Character Descriptions. (page 66)

- Comment on the quotes from the book. (page 67)

- Make a Cheese, Please! class recipe book. (page 68)

Student Poll

Do you believe in witches?   Yes   No

If you do believe in witches, do you think you could recognize a witch if you saw one?

                                                              Yes   No

A witch is:

good	or	bad	or	both
pretty	or	ugly	or	both
male	or	female	or	both
gentle	or	mean	or	both
funny	or	serious	or	both
friendly	or	scary	or	both

A witch travels by _____

A witch wears _____

A witch has _____

Draw a typical witch.

Witch Notes

As you read Chapters 1-4, make notes about what you learn about witches.

Appearances: _____

_____

_____

_____

Attitudes: _____

_____

Abilities: _____

_____

_____

Work in small groups and develop a plan for finding witches. How would you recognize one, and what would you do if you found one? Write down your ideas and then share them with the rest of the class. Discuss the merits of each plan.

_____

_____

_____

_____

_____

_____

Mouse Puzzle

Across

1. Mice have _____ eyes.
3. High-pitched sounds are used to _____ .
4. It is above average.
9. This state has a large rodent farm.
10. Since they sleep during the day, they are _____.
11. Mice that are active during the P.M. sleep during the _____.
13. The average life span is _____ years.
14. Their ears and nose are very _____.

Down

1. The tail is used for holding and _____.
2. This famous mouse was born in 1928.
5. Since their front teeth never stop growing, they must do this to keep them filed down.
6. The mouse is a _____.
7. North American mice came from this continent.
8. These are good for them to eat.
12. These help them to feel things.

Witches, Witches, Witches

Many stories include witches. Some of the most well-known are:

the good and bad witches of *The Wizard of Oz*   television witches

the witch in *Snow White*   the witch in *Hansel and Gretel*

Halloween witches   the witch in *Sleeping Beauty*

How are all these witches, including Dahl's witches and any others you would like to add, similar and different? List these attributes below. What conclusions can you draw about witches?

Similar Attributes:

Differing Attributes:

Stereotypes

What is the meaning of *stereotype?* _____

_____

Describe the stereotypes we have of:

witches _____

_____

grandmothers _____

_____

little boys _____

_____

Do the characters in *The Witches* fit the stereotypes?

Grandmamma:

Unique _____

Typical _____

Grand High Witch:

Unique _____

Typical _____

Storyteller—The Main Character:

Unique _____

Typical _____

Story Diagram

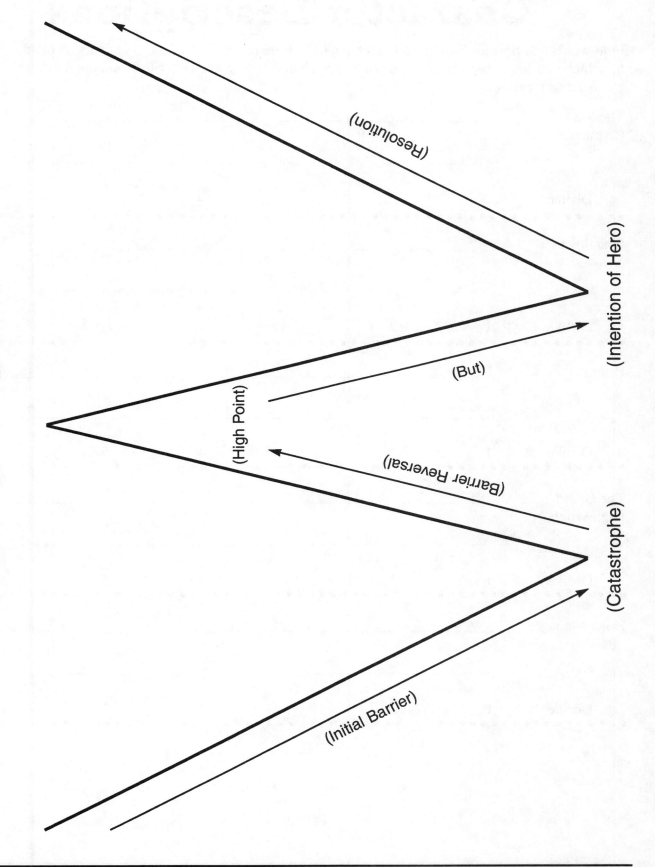

(Resolution)

(Intention of Hero)

(But)

(High Point)

(Barrier Reversal)

(Catastrophe)

(Initial Barrier)

Character Descriptions

Find words and phrases Dahl used to create a mental image of each of his characters. Note the page(s) on which you found the words. Then rate each character on a scale of 1 to 5 on how much you like the character as a person.

The Main
Character   _____

              _____

    Dislike   1   2   3   4   5   Like
• •

Grandmother   _____

              _____

    Dislike   1   2   3   4   5   Like
• •

Bruno   _____

              _____

    Dislike   1   2   3   4   5   Like
• •

The Grand
High Witch   _____

              _____

    Dislike   1   2   3   4   5   Like
• •

Hotel Manager   _____

              _____

    Dislike   1   2   3   4   5   Like
• •

What Do You Think?

Comment on the following quotes from the book:

For all you know, a witch might be living next door to you right now...she might even be your lovely school-teacher who is reading these words to you at this very moment. (page 10)

What a lovely secret silent place it was. (page 57)

...I might even suggest that they come and do a bit of cruelty-to-children preventing at my school. We could certainly use them here. (page 61)

It is always funny when you catch someone doing something coarse and she thinks no one is looking. (page 63)

There are times when something is so frightful you become mesmerized by it and can't look away. (page 66)

I don't know how long I had been there but it seemed like forever. The worst part of it was not being allowed to cough or make a sound, and knowing that if I did, I was as good as dead. (page 88)

...What's so wonderful about being a little boy anyway? Why is that necessarily any better than being a mouse? I know that mice get hunted and they sometimes get poisoned or caught in traps. But little boys sometimes get killed, too. Little boys can be run over by motor-cars or they can die of some awful illness. Little boys have to go to school. Mice don't. Mice don't have to pass exams. Mice don't have to worry about money. Mice, as far as I can see, have only two enemies, humans and cats. My grandmother is a human, but I know for certain that she will always love me whoever I am. And she never, thank goodness, keeps a cat. When mice grow up, they don't ever have to go to war and fight against other mice. Mice, I felt certain, all like each other. People don't. (pages 118-119)

She somehow managed to gather herself together enough to close the door. She leaned against it, staring down at me white-faced and shaking all over. I saw tears beginning to come out of her eyes and go dribbling down her cheeks. (page 126)

Children should never have baths, my grandmother said. It's a dangerous habit. (page 129)

Suddenly there I was swinging to and fro upside down. It was terrific. I loved it. This, I told myself, is how a trapeze artist in a circus must feel as he goes swishing through the air high up in the circus tent. (page 165)

Only the children in the room were really enjoying it. They all seemed to know instinctively that something good was going on right there in front of them, and they were clapping and cheering and laughing like mad. (page 187)

It doesn't matter who you are or what you look like so long as somebody loves you. (page 197)

...We shall do it entirely by ourselves, just you and me! That will be our work for the rest of our class! (page 208)

Cheese, Please!

Name: _____ 's Recipe for _____

Ingredients:

Procedure:

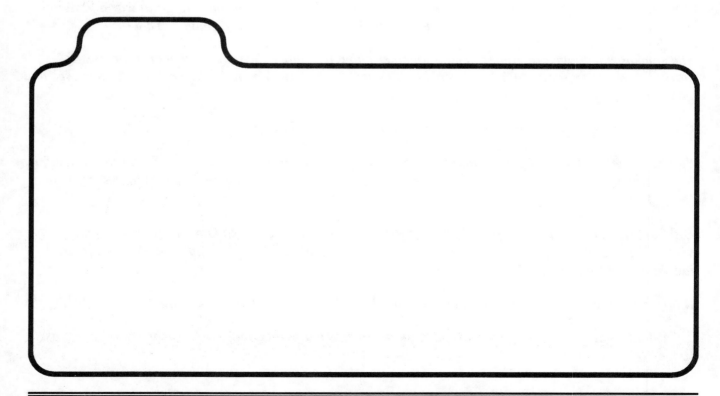

Matilda

by Roald Dahl

Matilda was a sensitive and brilliant little girl who had perfect speech at one-and-a-half years and had taught herself to read by the time she was three. Unfortunately, she had dim-witted parents and an older brother who treated her as if she were "nothing more than a scab." Her mother, Mrs. Wormwood, spent all her time playing bingo. Mr. Wormwood was a dishonest used car salesman who delighted in deceiving his customers for his personal financial gain. They both believed Matilda was a dunce and all the reading she did was a terrible waste of time.

However, being bright certainly gave Matilda the edge she needed to get her revenge on her parents for the despicable way they treated her. First, she made Mr. Wormwood's hat get stuck on his head with superglue. Then she scared her family by making them believe that their house was haunted. When her father acted in a really foul way, Matilda planned a trick to make him unknowingly bleach his hair blond. All of her little practical jokes at least made life a little more bearable.

Although her parents and homelife were wretched, Matilda found a friend and supporter in her kindergarten teacher, Miss Honey, when she started school. Miss Honey was wonderful and caring and wanted to help Matilda anyway she could. Unfortunately, Miss Honey could not get any help from the school's headmistress, Miss Trunchbull, who was one of the meanest people imaginable. Rather than help students learn, Miss Trunchbull seemed determined to destroy them. The children were helpless against her cruelty until Matilda miraculously developed a very special talent which gave them a little sweet revenge.

As Matilda got to know Miss Honey better, she learned that Miss Trunchbull's cruelty also extended to Miss Honey. Matilda could not tolerate this situation and decided to take action. She devised a plan that used her new talent to solve Miss Honey's problem, which led to a happy solution to her own life as well.

Matilda

Before the Book

- List the names of the main characters on the board and have students make predictions about each one's traits.
  — Matilda
  — Mr. and Mrs. Wormwood
  — Miss Trunchbull
  — Miss Honey
- Have students tell what clues they are using, especially taking into account Roald Dahl's style of writing.

During the Book

Questions listed under the chapters may be used for discussion, journal writing, or guided reading.

Section 1

Chapter "The Reading of Books":

- Find all the words and phrases Dahl used to describe Matilda that show what an extraordinary child she was.

  Examples:
  — sensitive
  — bright
  — brilliant
  — mind was so nimble
  — quick to learn
  — By the age of one-and-a-half her speech was perfect, and she knew as many words as most grown-ups.
  — By the time she was three, Matilda had taught herself to read.
- What do you think is Dahl's opinion of books? What books and authors does he recommend?

Chapter "Mr. Wormwood, the Great Car Dealer":

- Describe Mr. Wormwood. What is amusing about this family?
- Make combinations using cars from Mr. Wormwood's dealership. (page 72)

Section 2

Chapters "The Hat and the Superglue," "The Ghost," "Arithmetic," and "The Platinum Blond Man":

- What do you think about the tricks Matilda played on her father? Do you think she was justified? clever? satisfied? mean? bratty? funny?
- Using a conversion table, change British pounds to various foreign currency equivalents for the prices of Mr. Wormwood's cars. (page 73)

Matilda

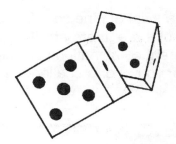

During the Book *(cont.)*

Section 3

Chapters "Miss Honey" and "The Trunchbull":
*   Practice math with dice Probability problems. (page 74–75)
*   Compare/contrast Miss Honey and Miss Trunchbull.

Chapter "The Parents":
*   What attitudes and opinions did Matilda's parents have that were in opposition to Miss Honey's values?

Section 4

Chapters "Throwing the Hammer" and "Bruce Bogtrotter and the Cake":
*   What do you think of what Hortensia had done in the past to Miss Trunchbull? How is Miss Trunchbull so powerful, physically and mentally?

Section 5

Chapters "Lavendar," "The Weekly Test," "The First Miracle," and "The Second Miracle":
*   What gave Lavendar the motivation to play a trick on Miss Trunchbull?
*   What was the miracle? Why do you think it happened?

Section 6

Chapters "Miss Honey's Cottage," Miss Honey's Story," and "The Names":
*   What was Miss Honey's amazing revelation?

Section 7

Chapters "The Practice," "The Third Miracle," and "A New Home":
*   How was playing this trick on Miss Trunchbull different from the tricks Matilda had played on her father?
*   What do you think of the ending of the story?
*   Play your own mind game by using a secret code. (page 76)

After the Book

*   Working in small groups, choose an incident that made you laugh and act it out for the rest of the class. Some funny episodes you might want to choose from are:
    — The hat and the superglue
    — The ghost in the chimney
    — Mr. Wormwood and the bleached hair
    — Miss Trunchbull and the newt
    — Miss Trunchbull and the mysterious chalk
*   Diagram the story of *Matilda*. (page 77)
*   Examine the characters and rate them. (page 78)
*   Comment on quotes from the book. (page 79)
*   Make a class recipe book of Honey Treats. (page 80)

Mr. Wormwood's Cars

Below is a list of nine cars found on Mr. Wormwood's Used Car Lot. If he were to sell them in groups of three, there are 84 possible combinations he could make. Can you make 30 of the 84 different combinations of three cars each? Use the abbreviations for ease. The first one is done for you. For a challenge make all 84.

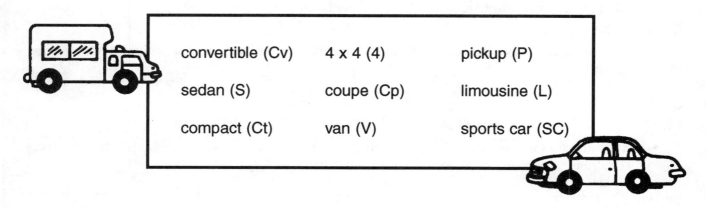

convertible (Cv)	4 x 4 (4)	pickup (P)
sedan (S)	coupe (Cp)	limousine (L)
compact (Ct)	van (V)	sports car (SC)

1. Cv, Cp, SC

2. _____

3. _____

4. _____

5. _____

6. _____

7. _____

8. _____

9. _____

10. _____

11. _____

12. _____

13. _____

14. _____

15. _____

16. _____

17. _____

18. _____

19. _____

20. _____

21. _____

22. _____

23. _____

24. _____

25. _____

26. _____

27. _____

28. _____

29. _____

30. _____

Currency Exchange Rates

Mr. Wormwood gives the prices of his cars in pounds. Use the currency rates listed below to compute the equivalent cost of his cars in other countries.

Fill in the amounts that are equivalent to the prices of Mr. Wormwood's cars.

	U.K. Pound 1.00	U.S. Dollar 1.49	Mexico Peso 4.68	Japan Yen 167.53	Italy Lira 2,524.10	Germany D-Mark 2.58	France F-Franc 8.78
1.	278.00						
2.	1,425.00						
3.	118.00						
4.	760.00						
5.	111.00						
6.	1,999.50						
7.	86.00						
8.	699.50						
9.	637.00						
10.	1,649.50						
11.	4,303.50						

Probability

Matilda is considered extraordinary because the chance of having a kindergarten student like Matilda is really quite small. Another word for chance is probability. Figuring out the actual probability requires knowing how many students like Matilda there are out of all the kindergarteners.

Use a pair of dice to practice figuring out probabilities. Imagine we have a white die and a black die.

Each die has six sides:

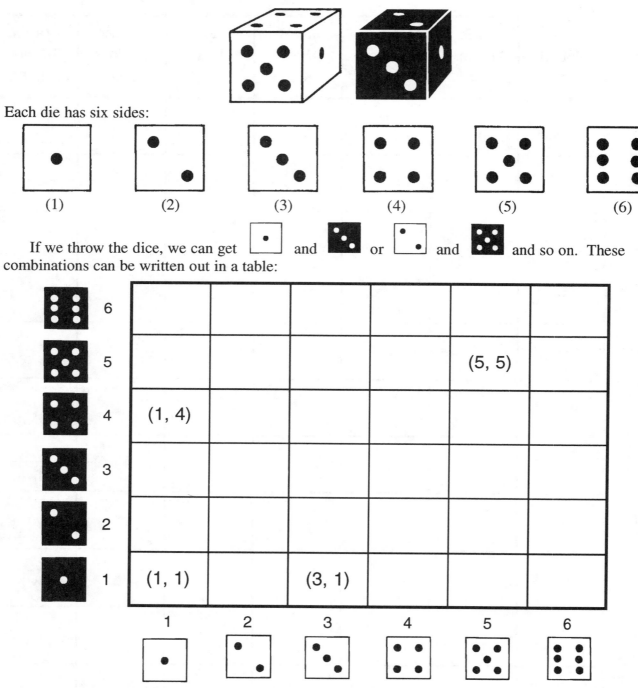

Some of the possible combinations have been filled in. Can you complete the table? (Be sure that you write the number for the die on the horizontal line first for each pair.)

Probability *(cont.)*

How many combinations are possible when you throw two dice? _____

Circle the pairs that total eight. How many did you circle? _____

The probability of throwing an eight would be five out of 36 because there are five combinations that add up to eight, and there are 36 possible combinations altogether. This can also be written as a fraction 5/36. If we use the fraction and divide five by 36, the probability can be written as .14.

Give the probability of the following by using the chart on page 74. Write your answers in three ways for each.

When throwing two dice, the probability of getting a sum of:

9 is _____   _____   _____

6 is _____   _____   _____

11 is _____   _____   _____

14 is _____   _____   _____

2 is _____   _____   _____

What is the probability of getting a product of:

20 _____   _____   _____

36 _____   _____   _____

12 _____   _____   _____

6 _____   _____   _____

1 _____   _____   _____

Secret Code Message

Only Miss Honey knew about Matilda's special power. If you have a friend with whom you share secrets, you may want to use a secret code to write messages to each other. Use the key below to figure out the message. Then write your answer in the secret code and give it to a classmate to decipher.

♋	♌	χ	♎	∩	φ	γ	♒	♓	φ	✳	λ	μ
a	**b**	**c**	**d**	**e**	**f**	**g**	**h**	**i**	**j**	**k**	**l**	**m**

ν	□	π	θ	♥	↔	↑	◆	√	∇	∅	⊕	⊆
n	**o**	**p**	**q**	**r**	**s**	**t**	**u**	**v**	**w**	**x**	**y**	**z**

∇♒♋↑   ♎□   ⊕□◆   ↑♒♓ν✳   ♒♋ππ∩ν∩♎
↑□   μ♓↔↔   ↑♥◆νχ♒♌◆λλ?

Write your response using the secret code. Then give it to a classmate.

_____

_____

_____

_____

Story Diagram

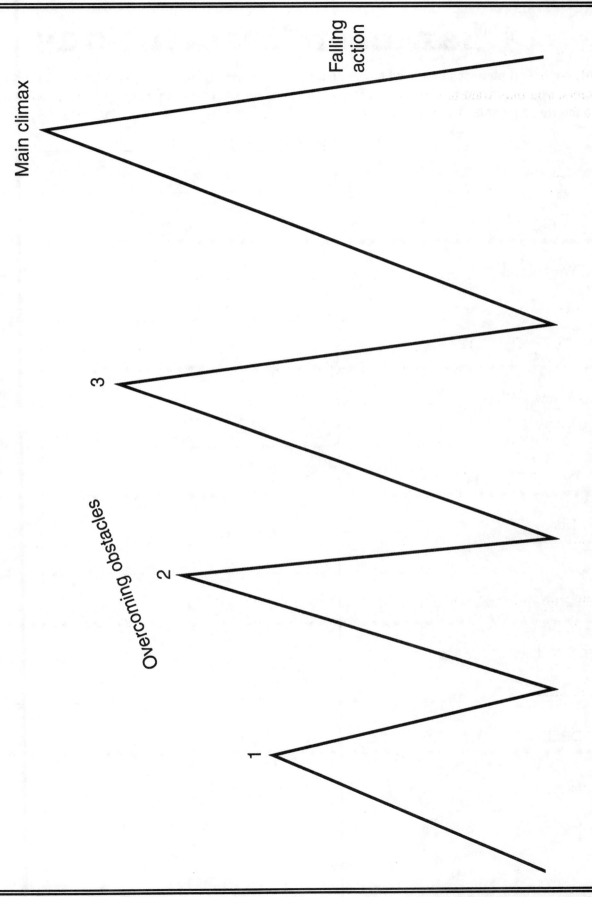

Main climax

Falling action

3

2

Overcoming obstacles

1

Character Descriptions

Find words and phrases Dahl used to create a mental image of each of his characters. Note the page(s) on which you found the words. Then rate each character on a scale of 1 to 5 on how much you like the character as a person.

Matilda _____

_____

Dislike   1   2   3   4   5   Like
•••

Mrs. Wormwood _____

_____

Dislike   1   2   3   4   5   Like
•••

Mr. Wormwood _____

_____

Dislike   1   2   3   4   5   Like
•••

Miss Honey _____

_____

Dislike   1   2   3   4   5   Like
•••

Miss Trunchbull _____

_____

Dislike   1   2   3   4   5   Like
•••

What Do You Think?

Comment on the following quotes from the book:

It's a funny thing about mothers and fathers. Even when their own child is the most disgusting little blister you could ever imagine, they still think that he or she is wonderful. (page 7)

...The way he tells it I feel I am right there on the spot watching it all happen.
"A fine writer will always make you feel that," Mrs. Phelps said. "And don't worry about the bits you can't understand. Sit back and allow the words to wash around you, like music." (page 19)

The books transported her into new worlds and introduced her to amazing people who lived exciting lives. (page 21)

"No one ever got rich being honest," the father said. (page 23)

"Do you think that all children's books ought to have funny bits in them?" Miss Honey asked. "I do." Matilda said. "Children are not so serious as grown-ups and they love to laugh." (page 81)

I'm not in favor of blue-stocking girls. A girl should think about making herself look attractive so she can get a good husband later on. Looks are more important than books, Miss Hunky...
"Now look at me," Mrs. Wormwood said. "Then look at you. You chose books. I chose looks."
(page 97)

They gazed in wonder at this goddess, and suddenly even the boil on her nose was no longer a blemish but a badge of courage. (page 108)

"That's the way to make them learn, Miss Honey," she said. "You take it from me, it's no good just telling them. You've got to hammer it into them. There's nothing like a little twisting and twiddling to encourage them to remember things. It concentrates their minds wonderfully." (page 155)

...The whole object of life, Headmistress, is to go forwards... (page 217)

...Your brain is for the first time having to struggle and strive and keep really busy, which is great... (page 230)

Honey Treats

Name: _____ 's Recipe for _____

Ingredients:

Procedure:

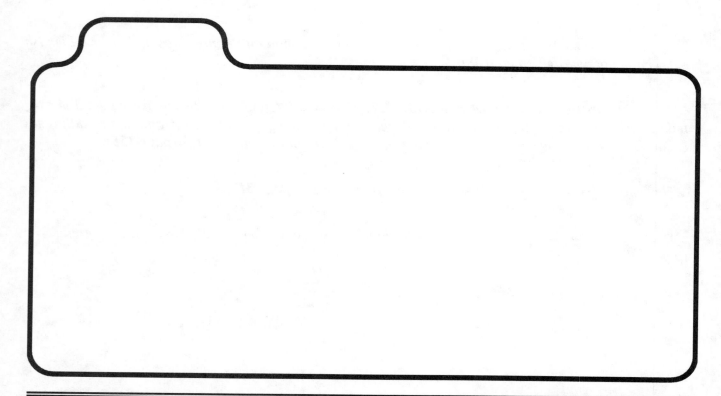

Boy Tales of Childhood

by Roald Dahl

Boy Tales of Childhood is Roald Dahl's account of his own childhood experiences. He first gives us some family history. His parents were from Norway but had moved to South Wales. When he was three years old, his seven-year-old sister died of appendicitis, and then his father died of pneumonia soon after. His mother was left with five children and one on the way. Because of his father's belief that English schools would provide a better education for his children than those in Norway, his mother decided to stay near England despite the hardship of her situation.

As Roald Dahl was growing up, many incidents left a lasting impression on him. There was the Great Mouse Plot in which he and his friends played a practical joke on a mean sweetshop owner and for which he was severely punished. Once his older sister took the family on a motor-car ride and crashed. Roald almost lost his nose! He remembers the family summer holidays in Norway and treating his older sister's fiancé to a special goat's tobacco smoke. At school the headmasters and older boys were cruel, but it was not all bad. He had a chance to help test new chocolate candies each year and became a star athlete and photographer.

Roald Dahl says that his book is not an autobiography. It is a recounting of those things that happened to him early in life that have "remained seared on my memory." These experiences give us a glimpse of the person behind the many children's books he wrote and explain where some of his ideas originated.

Boy Tales of Childhood

Before the Book

Read Roald Dahl's introduction together. Discuss how this book is different from an autobiography. Have students share experiences from their own lives that had a lasting impression.

During the Book

As students read the book, have them fill in the outline as a guide to help remember details about Dahl's life. (page 83)

Starting Point

Trace Papa's moves around Europe. (page 89)

Llandaff Cathedral School

Just as Thwaites told stories about the different candies, have students write their explanatory stories about the candies they eat today. (page 90)

St. Peter's

Discuss the importance of the students' tuck-boxes. Then have students consider what they might put into their own tuck-boxes. (page 91)

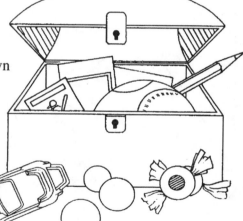

After the Book

- Play a board game to review Dahl's life. (pages 92–95)

- Complete the Dahl Puzzle. (page 96)

- Categorize Dahl's experiences under: funny, painful, unpleasant. (page 97)

- Look for possible relationships between experiences and his writing: characters, plots, events, values. (pages 98–99)

- Discuss the similarities and differences between Roald Dahl's school life and your own.

- Choose one incident from his life and write a letter about it to Roald Dahl as a friend.

- If Roald Dahl had been a boy today rather than in the 1920's and 1930's, how might his life have been different? What would not have changed? (page 100)

- Comment on the quotes taken from the book. (page 101)

- Make a Favorite Foods class recipe book. (page 102)

Fill-in Outline

I. Starting Point

   A. Papa

      1. Name:_____

      2. From: _____

      3. Occupation: _____

      4. Characteristics: _____

         a. _____

         b. _____

         c. _____

      5. Beliefs:_____

         a. _____

         b. _____

      6. Died: _____

   B. Mama

      1. Name:_____

      2. From: _____

      3. Characteristics: _____

         a. _____

         b. _____

   C. Siblings

      1. _____

      2. _____

      3. _____

      4. _____

      5. _____

   D. Kindergarten

      1. School: _____

      2. Exciting memory: _____

Fill-in Outline *(cont.)*

II. Llandaff Cathedral School, 1923-5 (ages 7-9)

   A. Two memories

      1. _____

      2. _____

         a. Candy examples:

            (1.) _____

            (2.) _____

            (3.) _____

            (4.) _____

            (5.) _____

         b. Owner:

            (1.) Name: _____

            (2.) Characteristics: _____

               (a.) _____

               (b.) _____

         c. Mouse Plot: _____

         d. Mr. Coombes: _____

            (1.) Position: _____

            (2.) Action taken: _____

   B. Summer holidays in Norway

      1. Journey there: _____

         a. Number of days: _____

         b. Number of people: _____

         c. Number of trunks: _____

Fill-in Outline *(cont.)*

    d. Transportation: _____

        (1.) _____

        (2.) _____

        (3.) _____

        (4.) _____

        (5.) _____

        (6.) _____

  2. Reunion:_____

    a. With: _____

    b. Feast: _____

  3. Magic island:

    a. _____

    b. _____

    c. _____

  4. Doctor's visit:

    a. Reason: _____

    b. Painful memory: _____

III. St. Peter's, 1925-9 (ages 9-13)

  A. Boarding school

    1. Tuck-box for: _____

    2. Writing home: _____

      a. When: _____

      b. Positive aspect: _____

      c. Negative aspect: _____

    3. The Matron:

      a. Where: _____

Fill-in Outline *(cont.)*

   b. Characteristics:

      (1.) _____

      (2.) _____

      (3.) _____

   c. Incidents:

      (1.) Wragg: _____

      (2.) Arkle: _____

      (3.) Tweedie: _____

      (4.) Homesickness: _____

        (a.) Plan: _____

        (b.) Dr. Dunbar: _____

B. A motor-car drive

   1. Driver: _____

   2. Car:

     a. Type: _____

     b. Description: _____

   3. The ride:

     a. _____

     b. _____

C. Captain Hardcastle

   1. Appearance:

     a. _____

     b. _____

     c. _____

     d. _____

   2. Prep:

     a. Rule: _____

Fill-in Outline *(cont.)*

    b. Roald's problem: _____

    c. Stripe:

       (1.) Consequence: _____

       (2.) Highton's friendship: _____

D. Little Ellis

   1. Ailment: _____

   2. Procedure: _____

   3. Reason: _____

E. Half-sister's fiancé

   1. Feelings towards him: _____

   2. His habit: _____

   3. The practical joke: _____

IV. Repton and Shell, 1929-36 (ages 13-20)

  A. Repton School

    1. Repton School:

      a._____

      b. _____

      c. _____

    2. Boazers:

      a. Who: _____

      b. What they did: _____

    3. The Headmaster:

      a. Description: _____

      b. Became: _____

      c. Doubts: _____

Fill-in Outline *(cont.)*

B. Chocolate testers

    1. Company: _____

    2. The task: _____

    3. Imagined: _____

    4. Basis for: _____

C. Corkers

    1. Who: _____

    2. Description: _____

D. Fagging

    1. Definition: _____

    2. Dahl's job: _____

E. Games and photography

    1. Eton-fives description:

        a. _____

        b. _____

    2. Captain:

        a. _____

        b. _____

    3. Photography:

        a. Arthur Norris: _____

        b. After leaving school: _____

F. Goodbye school

    1. Dahl's choice: _____

    2. Shell Company:

        a. Job: _____

        b. 1939: _____

Map of Europe

On the map below, locate:

> Oslo, Norway
> Cardiff, South Wales
> Weston-super-Mare, England
> Calais, Paris, and La Rochelle, France.

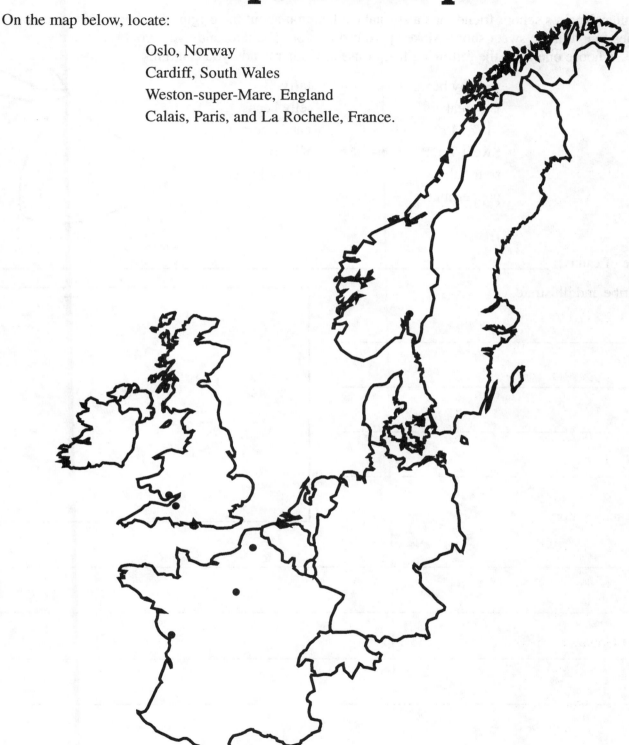

After filling in the names of each city, show the path of Harold Dahl's moves during his early years with a red crayon.

Candy

Thwaites, Roald's school friend, had a special explanation about the origin of many of the various candies found in the sweet shop. Make up your own story about a candy you would find in a store today. Choose one from the following list, or use any other candy you can think of:

gummy bears   taffy

jawbreakers   jelly beans

M & M's®   candy corn

Sweet Tarts®   Kisses®

sour balls   peanut butter cup

peppermint

Name of candy: _____

Describe and illustrate it:

_____

_____

_____

The candy's story:

_____

_____

_____

_____

Tuck-Box

Add your name to the top of the tuck-box, and at the bottom of the page tell what personal treasures you would put inside it.

_____

_____

_____

_____

_____

_____

_____

_____

_____

_____

Summer

Take a trip from South Wales to Norway. Using the question cards on page 94–95, answer each question correctly, roll a die, and move your marker. The first person to reach Norway is the winner!

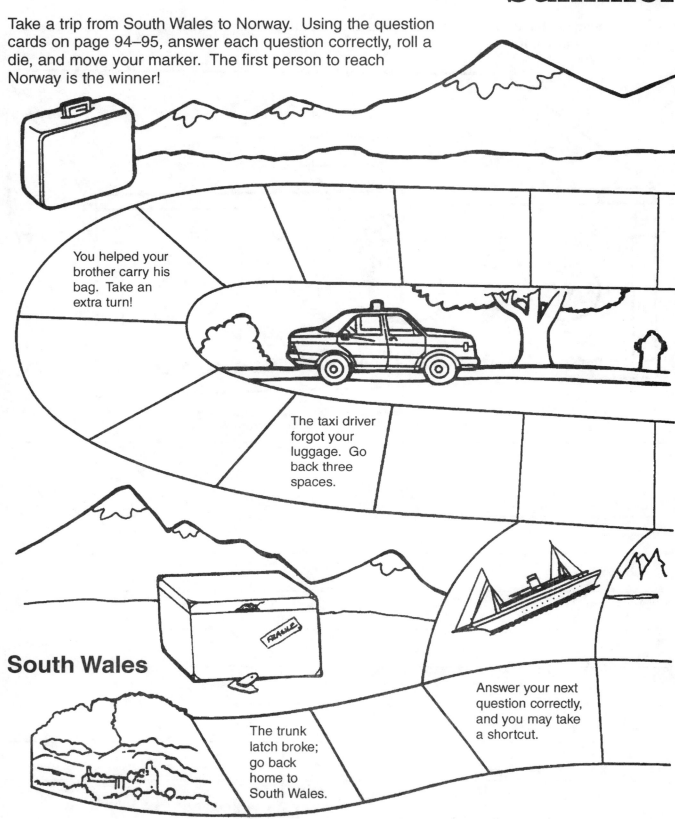

You helped your brother carry his bag. Take an extra turn!

The taxi driver forgot your luggage. Go back three spaces.

South Wales

The trunk latch broke; go back home to South Wales.

Answer your next question correctly, and you may take a shortcut.

Holiday *(cont.)*

Norway

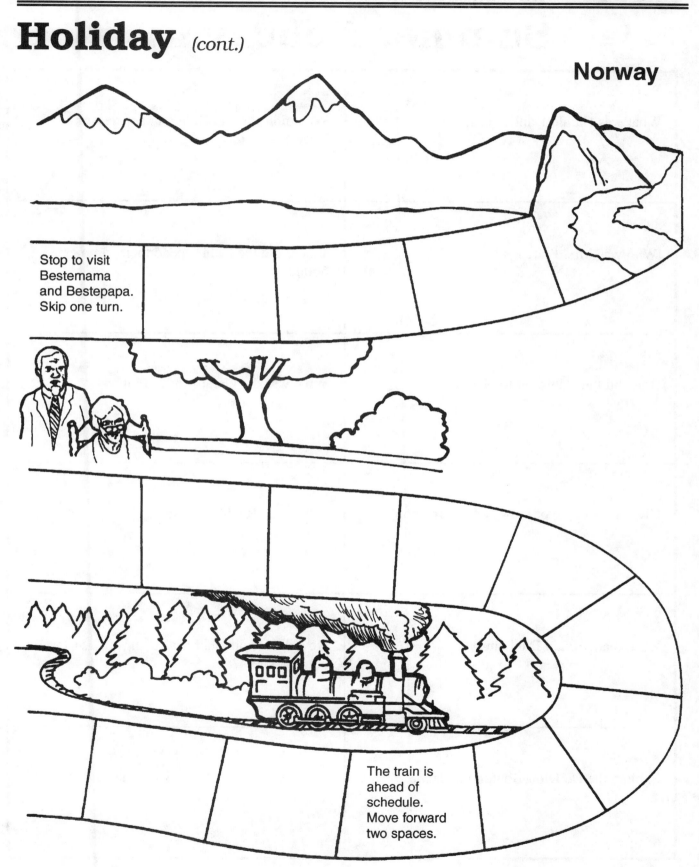

Stop to visit
Bestemama
and Bestepapa.
Skip one turn.

The train is
ahead of
schedule.
Move forward
two spaces.

Summer Holiday *(cont.)*

1. What was Harald Dahl's occupation?	**2.** Why didn't Roald Dahl's father return to Norway?
3. Who was Mrs. Pratchett?	**4.** Where did the Dahls spend their summer holidays?
5. How did the Dahls get to Norway?	**6.** What was the Great Mouse Plot?
7. Give an example of bravery from the book.	**8.** When was Roald Dahl scared?
9. What made Roald Dahl angry?	**10.** How did Roald Dahl deal with homesickness?
11. Explain the De Dion-Bouton incident.	**12.** What did Captain Hardcastle do?

Summer Holiday *(cont.)*

13. What was Goat's tobacco?	14. How did Roald Dahl get the idea for *Charlie and the Chocolate Factory?*
15. Who was Corkers?	16. Name the four interests Roald Dahl had at Repton School.
17. Why didn't Roald Dahl go to Oxford or Cambridge?	18. Where did Shell Company send Roald Dahl?
19. What did the headmaster of Repton School eventually become?	20. Name a major improvement in medicine since Roald Dahl's days.
21. What did Roald Dahl learn to do at his first school that he continued to do throughout his growing years?	22. What was "fagging"?
23. (Write in your own question.)	24. (Write in your own question.)

Dahl Puzzle

Directions: Complete the puzzle below. Can you find the surprise hidden in the completed puzzle?

1. Although born in Wales, Roald Dahl was _____ by descent.

2. Roald Dahl's great idea for Mrs. Pratchett was _____.

3. The headmasters used a _____ for punishment.

4. He spent his summer _____ in Norway.

5. A tuck-box was used for storing _____.

6. The type of automobile his sister drove was a _____.

7. The sister's fiancé unknowingly smoked _____.

8. The boys of Repton annually tasted Cadbury's® _____ .

9. After graduation, Roald Dahl went to work for _____.

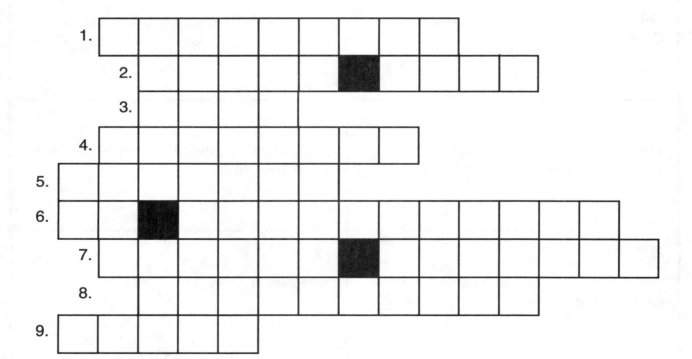

Memories of Childhood

Referring to his memories of childhood, Roald Dahl said: "Some are funny. Some are painful. Some are unpleasant."

Look over the outline you filled in as you read the book and categorize the events under the appropriate headings. Do some things belong in more than one category? Add your own headings if you like.

Funny   **Painful**

_____   _____

_____   _____

_____   _____

_____   _____

_____   _____

_____   _____

Unpleasant

_____

_____

_____

_____

_____

_____

_____

_____

Boyhood Experiences

Below are listed some events/characters from Dahl's other books. Under each one, write an experience he tells about in *Boy Tales of Childhood* that may have given him the idea for it.

James and the Giant Peach

> James's great adventure across the ocean

_____

Charlie and the Chocolate Factory

> Willie Wonka was the great inventor of chocolates.

_____

Danny, the Champion of the World

> Danny driving the Baby Austin

_____

When Danny came home from school, his father was so angry about learning that Danny's teacher had hit him with a cane that he was going to go right over and beat him up.

_____

Captain Lancaster

_____

Danny being accused of cheating in class

_____

Sergeant Samways' peculiar habit of putting an "h" in front of some words

_____

Danny's relationship with his father

_____

Boyhood Experiences *(cont.)*

The Witches

Grandmother

_____

Summer Norwegian holidays

_____

The witches' sweet shops

_____

Children being changed into mice

_____

Matilda

Miss Trunchbull

_____

The practical jokes that Matilda played to get back at people who were mean to her

_____

Can you think of any other relationships between his stories and his real life?

_____

_____

_____

_____

_____

A Change of Time

If Roald Dahl had been a boy growing up today rather than in the 1920's and 1930's, how might his life have been different? What would not have changed? Will we still be able to enjoy the same kinds of stories in the future?

What Do You Think?

Comment on the following quotes from the book:

His theory was that if the eye of a pregnant woman was constantly observing the beauty of nature, this beauty would somehow become transmitted to the mind of the unborn baby within her womb and that baby would grow up to be a lover of beautiful things. This was the treatment that all of his children received before they were born. (page 19)

Truth is more important than modesty. I must tell you, therefore, that it was I and I alone who had the idea for the great and daring Mouse Plot. We all have our moments of brilliance and glory, and this was mine. (page 35)

All grown-ups appear as giants to small children. (page 41)

When I recovered and went home, I was given this vast collection of my letters, all so neatly bound with green tape, more than six hundred of them altogether, dating from 1925 to 1945, each one in its original envelope with the old stamps still on them. I am awfully lucky to have something like this to refer to in my old age. (page 82)

...I was always able to draw an imaginary line from my bed to our house over in Wales. Never once did I go to sleep looking away from my family. It was a great comfort to do this. (page 90)

Homesickness is a bit like seasickness. You don't know how awful it is till you get it, and when you do, it hits you right in the top of the stomach and you want to die. The only comfort is that both homesickness and seasickness are instantly curable. The first goes away the moment you walk out of the school grounds and the second is forgotten as soon as the ship enters port. (page 93)

They were tough, those masters, make no mistake about it, and if you wanted to survive, you had to become pretty tough yourself. (page 113)

Pain was something we were expected to endure. Anesthetics and pain-killing injections were not much used in those days. Dentists, in particular, never bothered with them. But I doubt very much if you would be entirely happy today if a doctor threw a towel in your face and jumped on you with a knife. (pages 126-127)

Do you wonder then that this man's behavior used to puzzle me tremendously? He was an ordinary clergyman at that time as well as being Headmaster, and I would sit in the dim light of the school chapel and listen to him preaching about the lamb of God and about Mercy and Forgiveness and all the rest of it and my young mind would become totally confused. I knew very well that only the night before this preacher had shown neither Forgiveness nor Mercy in flogging some small boy who had broken the rules. (page 146)

The life of a writer is absolute hell compared with life of a businessman. The writer has to force himself to work. He has to make his own hours and if he doesn't go to his desk at all there is nobody to scold him. If he is a writer of fiction he lives in a world of fear. Each new day demands new ideas and he can never be sure whether he is going to come up with them or not....His only comprehension is absolute freedom. He has no master except his own soul, and that, I am sure, is why he does it. (page 171)

Favorite Foods

Name: _____'s Recipe for _____

Ingredients:

Procedure:

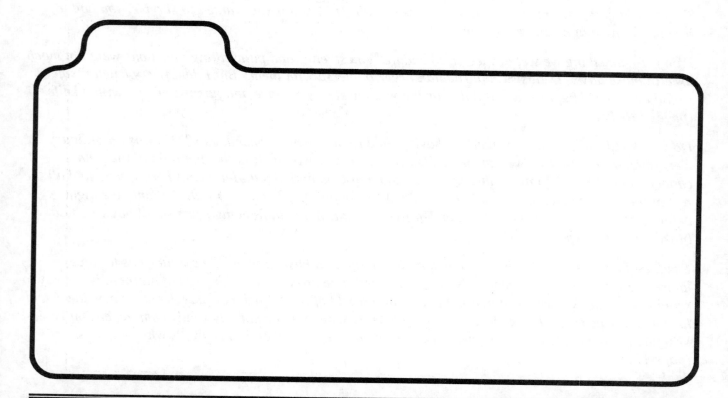

Culminating Activities

Using All the Books:

- Dahl's style of writing includes the use of exaggeration, frankness, and absurdity to create humor and mixing fact with fantasy to tell a story. Find two examples of each type of humor and one example of fact and fantasy from each book. (page 104)

- Look over the character descriptions from all of Dahl's books. Use your imagination and draw a picture of one of them. Hang the pictures near the one of Roald Dahl in your classroom display.

- Find examples from his books to support his ideas about what a children's author must do. (page 105)

- Comment on Dahl's philosophy about what he believes to be the most important function of books. (page 106)

- Working in small groups, act out a favorite scene from one of the books.

- Write a book review on one of the books.

- Create a TV commercial or magazine ad to promote one of the books.

- Draw a scene from one of the stories.

- Have a group debate about which book is the best, giving supporting reasons for the choice.

- Have pairs of students play a hangman type game using words, character names, and descriptive phrases from Dahl's works.

- Compare Roald Dahl to other familiar children's authors.

Style

Roald Dahl loves to make his readers laugh. He does this by using **exaggeration, frankness,** and **absurdity. Exaggeration** is a statement in which something is made much greater or worse than it really is. **Frankness** is saying something that most people are usually too shy to say. **Absurdity** is describing something that is so illogical that it probably would not happen in real life.

Think about all the books by Dahl that you have read. Find two examples of each type of humor. List them along with the book.

Exaggeration

Book _____

Example 1 _____

Example 2 _____

Frankness

Book _____

Example 1 _____

Example 2 _____

Absurdity

Book _____

Example 1 _____

Example 2 _____

Another technique Dahl uses is mixing fact with fantasy in his stories. Find an example of this combination from each of the fiction books you have read. If you need more room continue on the back.

_____

_____

_____

Dahl's Story Ingredients

About writing for children, Roald Dahl has said:

"...Children love violence — they are naturally aggressive. It baffles me that many adults do not realize this."

"I believe that the writer for children must be a jokey sort of a fellow, if you see what I mean by that. He must like simple tricks and jokes and riddles and other childish things. He must be unconventional and inventive. He must have a really first-class plot. He must know what enthralls children and what bores them. They love being spooked. They love suspense. They love action. They love ghosts. They love the finding of treasure. They love chocolates and toys and money. They love music. They love being made to giggle. They love seeing the villain meet a grisly death. They love a hero and they love the hero to be a winner. But they hate descriptive passages and flowery prose. They hate long descriptions of any sort. Many of them are sensitive to good writing and can spot a clumsy sentence. They like stories that contain a threat..."

- Find examples from the books you have read that support his ideas about children's stories.

Violence: _____

Tricks: _____

Jokes: _____

Riddles: _____

Unconventional: _____

Inventive: _____

Scary: _____

Suspense: _____

Action: _____

Ghosts: _____

Treasure: _____

Chocolates/toys/money: _____

Magic: _____

Funny: _____

Threat: _____

Villain punished: _____

Winning hero: _____

Dahl's Purpose

Dahl said that the most important function of his books is to get children to read. He believed that to be a successful children's book writer, he must create a story *that is so absorbing, exciting, funny, fast, and beautiful that the child will fall in love with it. And that first love affair between the young child and the young book will lead hopefully to other loves for other books and when this happens the battle is probably won. The child will have found a crock of gold.*

Comment on Dahl's philosophy. Do you agree with his ideas? Do you think he achieved his goal?

Roald Dahl Festival

Have a Roald Dahl Festival in which you share the books you have read with students of other classrooms. Invite other classes to view:

- A display of your work
  — Character pictures
  — Research projects
  — Recipe books
- Reader's Theater presentations
  — Dahl's poems
  — Key conversations
  — Favorite scenes
- Make and serve refreshments using recipes from the class recipe books.
- Have students share something they learned about Roald Dahl.
  — His life
  — His writing style
  — His philosophies

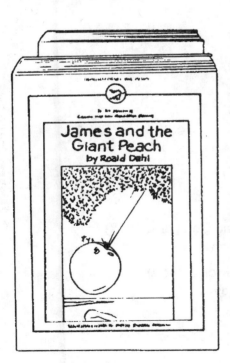 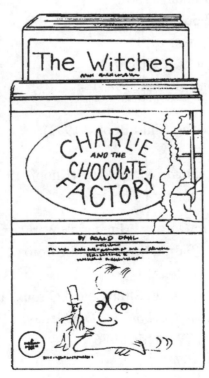 

Bibliography

Books by Roald Dahl:

The BFG (Farrar, Strauss, and Giroux, 1982)

Boy Tales of Childhood (Puffin, 1986)

Charlie and the Chocolate Factory (Puffin, 1988)

Charlie and the Great Glass Elevator (Knopf, 1972)

The Complete Adventures of Charlie and Mr. Willy Wonka (omnibus) (Allen and Unwin, 1978)

The Dahl Diary (Puffin, 1992)

Danny, the Champion of the World (Puffin, 1988)

Dirty Beasts (Farrar, Strauss, and Giroux, 1984)

The Enormous Crocodile (Knopf, 1978)

Esoi Trot (Puffin, 1992)

Fantastic Mr. Fox (Knopf, 1970)

George's Marvelous Medicine (Knopf, 1982)

The Giraffe and the Pelly and Me (Farrar, Strauss, and Giroux, 1985)

Going Solo (Farrar, Strauss, and Giroux, 1986)

The Gremlins (Random House, 1943)

James and the Giant Peach (Bantam, 1961)

The Magic Finger (Harper, 1966)

The Minpins (Viking Child Books, 1991)

Rhyme Stew (Viking Child Books, 1990)

Roald Dahl's Revolting Rhymes (Knopf, 1983)

The Twits (Knopf, 1981)

The Vicar of Nibbleswicke (Viking Child Books, 1992)

The Witches (Puffin, 1990)

The Wonderful Story of Henry Sugar & Six More (Knopf, 1977)

Related Stories:

Allamand, Pascale. *Cocoa Beans to Daisies.* (Frederick Warner and Company, 1978)

Babbitt, Natalie. *Kneeknock Rise.* (Farrar, Strauss, and Giroux, 1970)

Babbitt, Natalie. *The Search for Delicious.* (Farrar, Strauss, and Giroux, 1969)

Babbitt, Natalie. *Tuck Everlasting.* (Farrar, Strauss, and Giroux, 1975)

Banks, Lynne Reid. *The Indian in the Cupboard.* (Doubleday, 1980)

Baum, L. Frank. *The Wizard of Oz.* (Western, 1986)

Blume, Judy. *Freckle Juice.* (Dell, 1971)

Burnett, Frances Hodgson. *The Secret Garden.* (Penguin, 1987)

Butterworth, Oliver. *The Enormous Egg.* (Little, 1956)

Carroll, Lewis. *Alice's Adventures in Wonderland.* (Puffin, 1946)

Bibliography *(cont.)*

Related Stories *(cont.)*

Du Bois, William Pene. *The Twenty-One Balloons.* (Penguin, 1986)

Grahame, Kenneth. *The Wind in the Willows.* (Scribner, 1908)

Juster, Norton. *The Phantom Tollbooth.* (Ransom House, 1961)

Kingsley, Charles. *The Water Babies.* (Puffin, 1984)

Lawson, Robert. *Rabbit Hill.* (Penguin, 1944)

L'Engle, Madeleine. *A Wrinkle in Time.* (Dell, 1976)

Lewis, C.S. *The Lion, the Witch, and the Wardrobe.* (Macmillan, 1950)

Mitgutsch, Ali. *From Cocoa Bean to Chocolate.* (Carolrhoda Books, Inc., 1975)

Norton, Mary. *The Borrowers.* (Harcourt, 1953)

Paterson, Katherine. *Bridge to Terabithia.* (Harper and Row, 1987)

Pearce, Philippa. *Tom's Midnight Garden.* (Harper, 1984)

Perl, Lila. *The Great Ancestor Hunt.* (Clarion Books, 1989)

White, E.B. *Charlotte's Web.* (Harper, 1952)

Wolfman, Ira. *Do People Grow on Family Trees?* (Workman Publishing, 1991)

Resource Books:

Ammon, Richard. *The Kids' Book of Chocolate.* (Atheneum, 1987)

Chevalier, Tracy, ed. *Twentieth-Century Children's Writers, 3rd Edition.* (St. James Press, 1989)

Commire, Anne, ed. *Something About the Author, Volume 26.* (Gale Research, Inc., 1982)

Evory, Ann, ed. *Contemporary Authors, New Revision Series, Volume 6.* (Gale Research, Inc., 1982)

Hahn, James and Lynn. *Hamsters, Gerbils, Guinea Pigs, Pet Mice & Pet Rats.* (Franklin Watts, 1977)

Jacobson, Willard J. and Bergman, Abby B. *Science Activities for Children.* (Prentice Hall, 1983)

Kaufman, Joe. *What Makes It Go? What Makes It Work? What Makes It Fly? What Makes It Float?* (Golden Press, 1971)

Loewer, Peter. *The Inside–Out Stomach: An Introduction to Animals Without Backbones.* (Atheneum, 1990)

Olendorf, Donna, ed. *Something About the Author, Volume 65.* (Gale Research, Inc., 1991)

Wiessinger, John R. *Bugs, Slugs, and Crayfish - - Right Before Your Eyes.* (Enslow Publishers, 1989)

Answer Key

Pages 16-17
(Replicate drawings of bugs)

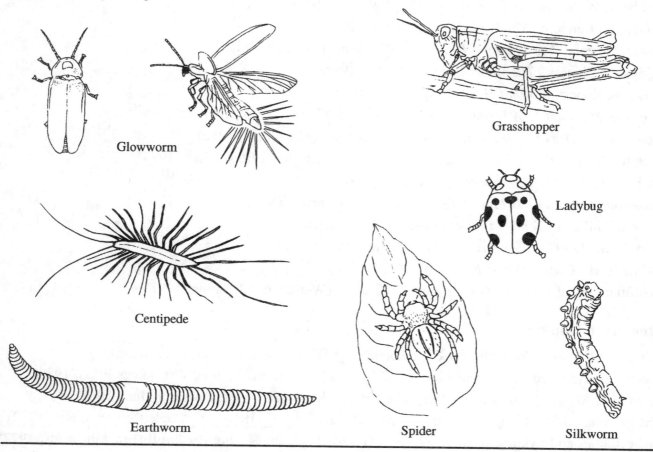

Glowworm

Grasshopper

Centipede

Ladybug

Earthworm

Spider

Silkworm

Page 34
Reading books is like taking a great glass elevator ride to near or distant places where you'll meet all kinds of characters. Be sure to take along a Wonka chocolate bar to enjoy along the way.

Page 36
Augustus fell into the chocolate river when he tried to drink from it.
Violet chewed the special chewing gum meal.
Veruca tried to grab a nut cracking squirrel and was caught instead.
Mike jumped into the special TV sending camera.
Charlie was the last one left on the tour.
Possible lessons:
Augustus - dangers of being greedy.
Violet - Constantly chewing gum is not attractive.
Veruca - You can't have everything and anything whenever you want it.
Mike - Too much TV is not good for you.
Charlie - Living a morally good life will be rewarded.

Pages 38-39
(Accept any answers written as Charlie Bucket might have answered.)
I. Chocolate candy: product: Wonka Chocolates.
Sell chocolate candy for a profit.
II. Boys and girls: it tastes good.
III. In town; vats, mixers, melters; cacao beans, milk, nuts, sugar, wrapping paper. etc.; people to do the mixing, pouring, wrapping, inspecting.
IV. Stores; TV commercials, newspaper ads; inventing rooms, other factories.
V. Grandpa Joe, Mom and Dad: Grandpa - ideas, Mom - tasting and testing, Dad - supervision.
VI. (Best guess)

Answer Key *(cont.)*

Page 40
Problems: Charlie and his family are very poor, Willie Wonka must stay in business.
Goals: Get enough to eat and stay alive; find a successor for Wonka.
Event 1: Wonka offers Golden Tickets.
Event 2: Charlie finds one.
Event 3: Other children disappear one by one.
Event 4: Charlie is left and offered the factory.
Resolution: Charlie and his family live comfortably for the rest of their lives;
Wonka Chocolate Factory will continue.

Page 49
1. 2.17 hours
2. .26 hours or 15.6 minutes; .16 hours or 9.75 minutes.
3. About 55 m.p.h. (89 km)
4. Yes. .54 hours
5. 8 m.p.h. (13 km)

Page 53
Main Idea: Danny is able to do the impossible
Who?: Danny and his dad
(Did) What?: Poached 120 pheasants from Hazell's Woods
When?: Just before Hazell's big shooting party in October
Where?: Hazell's Woods
How?: Putting the pheasants to sleep
Why?: Mr. Hazell was selfish and rude

Page 62

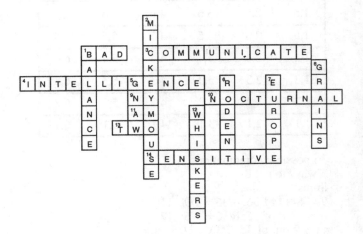

Page 65
Intention of Hero: Rid the world of witches.
Initial Barrier: Witches are disguised
Barrier Reversal: Grandmamma knows how to recognize a witch.
High Point: The boy finds out the witches' plan.
But: He gets caught.
Catastrophe: He is turned into a mouse.
Resolution: He is able to turn the witches into mice.

Page 73

Pound 1.00	Dollar 1.49	Peso 4.68	Yen 167.53	Lira 2,524.10	D-Mark 2.58	F-Franc 8.78
278.00	414.22	1,301.04	46,573.34	701,699.80	717.24	2,440.84
1,425.00	2,123.25	6,669.00	238,730.25	3,596,842.50	3,676.50	12,511.50
118.00	175.82	552.24	19,768.54	297,843.80	304.44	1,036.04
760.00	1,132.40	3,556.80	127,322.80	1,918,316.00	1,960.80	6,672.80
111.00	165.39	519.48	18,595.83	280,175.10	286.38	974.58
1,999.50	2,979.26	9,357.66	334,976.24	5,046,937.95	5,158.71	17,555.61
86.00	128.14	402.48	14,407.58	217,072.60	221.88	755.08
699.50	1,042.26	3,273.66	117,187.24	1,765,607.95	1,804.71	6,141.61
637.00	949.13	2,981.16	106,716.61	1,607,851.70	1,643.46	5,592.86
1,649.50	2,457.76	7,719.66	276,340.74	4,163,502.95	4,255.71	14,482.61
4,303.50	6,412.22	20,140.38	720,965.36	10,862,464.35	11,103.03	37,784.73

Answer Key *(cont.)*

Pages 74-75

1,6	2,6	3,6	4,6	5,6	6,6
1,5	2,5	3,5	4,5	5,5	6,5
1,4	2,4	3,4	4,4	5,4	6,4
1,3	2,3	3,3	4,3	5,3	6,3
1,2	2,2	3,2	4,2	5,2	6,2
1,1	2,1	3,1	4,1	5,1	6,1

36 possible combinations
5 ways to get 8
Sums:
9 = 4 out of 36; 4/36 = 1/9; .11
6 = 6 out of 36; 6/36 = 1/6; .17
11 = 2 out of 36; 2/36 = 1/18; . 06
14 = 0
2 = 1 out of 36; 1/36; .03
Products:
20 = 2 out of 36; 2/36 = 1/18; .06
36 = 1 out of 36; 1/36; .03
12 = 4 out of 36; 4/36 = 1/9; .11
6 = 4 out of 36; 4/36 = 1/9; .11
1 = 0

Page 76
What do you think happened to Miss Trunchbull?

Page 77
Obstacle 1: Rude, dim-witted parents.
Obstacle 2: Miss Trunchbull's cruelty to students.
Obstacle 3: Miss Trunchbull's cruelty to Miss Honey.
Main Climax: Matilda scares off Miss Trunchbull.
Falling Action: Matilda gets to live with Miss Honey.

Page 96

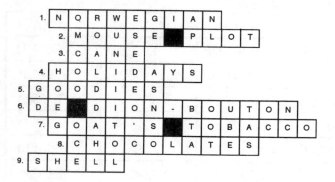

Pages 92-95
Answers to question cards:
1. Shipbroker
2. He always wanted to have his children educated in England.
3. Owner of the candy shop.
4. Norway
5. By train, taxis, boat
6. Roald and his friends put a dead mouse in Mrs. Pratchett's candy jar.
7. Various
8. Various
9. Cruel and unjustified treatment of school boys
10. Pretended to have appendicitis
11. Big sister drove the family in a car and crashed, cutting Roald's nose off.
12. Accused Roald of lying and cheating
13. Goat's droppings put into fiance's pipe
14. Testers for Cadbury® came to Repton School each year.
15. Unusual math teacher
16. Eton-fives, squash, football, and photography
17. He wanted to work for a company that would send him to faraway countries.
18. Africa
19. Archbishop of Canterbury
20. Anesthesia
21. Write letters consistently.
22. Being a lower classman servant to an upper classman